SURVIVAL COMMUNICATION:
Writing and Speaking for
Law Enforcement Officers

Special Agent
Stephen D. Gladis
Education/Communication Arts Unit
FBI Academy
Quantico, Virginia

All author's proceeds go to Heroes Inc., which financially supports the education of slain law enforcement officers' children.

Kendall/Hunt
Publishing Company
Dubuque, Iowa

Copyright © 1987 by Stephen D. Gladis

Library of Congress Catalog Card Number: 86–82511

ISBN 0–8403–4151–2

Printed in the United States of America

10 9 8 7 6 5 4 3 2

Dedication

To Steven and Margaret Gladis, my father and mother, who strived to support, guide, and educate me, and without whom this book would not exist.

Contents

Acknowledgments

To my wife Donna for her friendship, support, and love. To Pat Solley for her editorial excellence and enduring sense of humor. To John Hess for his friendship and wise counsel. And to the men and women in the FBI National Academy program for whom it has been an honor and a pleasure for me to serve.

Foreword

In law enforcement, as in many other occupational fields, success on the street as well as within the organization depends on the individual's ability to communicate effectively. Unfortunately, our ability to communicate with one another is something that we often take for granted. Consequently, most of us are not as adept as we could, or should, be in the area of written and oral communications. It is no exaggeration to state that the ability to communicate effectively is the single most important attribute of a law enforcement officer. In the worst case, the inability to communicate effectively or to correctly interpret messages received can lead to serious injury or death to the officer involved. However, while not every communications mistake leads to confrontation, most can have an impact on effectiveness, public relations, and eventually self-confidence.

It is also important for law enforcement agencies to recognize that effective communication, in all of its forms, is basic to the success of the organization. Most organizational problems have their root cause in communication failure. Success, conversely, can be attributed to effective communication on the part of all personnel involved. Thus it is in the best interest of an organization to insist that the quality of communication, both internally and externally, be of the highest order. This is easier said than done.

While communications skills are both subtle and complex in theory and practice, they are easily mastered by anyone willing to learn, and this book can help. Survival Communication focuses primarily on public speaking and writing. Both are fundamental skills and while they are not critical to officer survival from an operational standpoint, they are from an administrative one. Thus anyone interested in administrative advancement within the law enforcement organization would be well served to master both the written and spoken word. Mr. Gladis' book will serve the reader well in this regard.

> Edward J. Tully
> Chief
> Education/Communication Arts Unit
> FBI Academy

Introduction

1

For over 50 years law enforcement officers from across the United States have attended the FBI National Academy program (NA). These officers have all had one thing in common: they have come to the Academy to learn skills that will facilitate their professional growth. The success they find here is confirmed statistically. We know that one in seven will direct a department in the years to come, and that the upper ranks of law enforcement agencies across America will be filled by many of the others.

Without hesitation, most NA students agree that to be successful in their departments, they must be able to speak and write clearly and effectively. As a result, the Education/Communication Arts Unit at the Academy developed courses in the National Academy program that responded to those needs. First, the unit developed a course entitled "Effective Communications" to focus on effective public speaking, particularly on informing, persuading, and using nonverbal communication. While teaching this course, I was frequently asked by students for handout materials that they could take back to their departments and training officers. Based on these requests and on a general need I saw in the profession, I wrote several magazine articles relevant to public speaking. Two of these have appeared in publications, and two are new. All four relate directly to public speaking and outline some of the essentials taught in the National Academy program.

Second, the unit more recently has developed a course entitled "Survival Writing" which focuses on writing as a process and uses innovative techniques to improve police officers' writing skills. As with the speaking course, demands for handouts and requests from the field prompted me to write about writing. I have since written a series of articles, most of which have been published, that explain the writing process and outline strategies which will help the doubtful writer to improve quickly.

This book brings all these articles together for the first time. Police officers can now find under one cover instruction on speaking and writing that is specifically geared to them. Now those who do not get the opportunity to attend the National Academy need not miss the skills that are taught there.

The book is divided into three sections. The first section on **WRITING** sets forth some of the current theory of and practice in effective writing. Chapter 2, "Process Writing," outlines the basic steps in the writing process and provides the reader with a good, general overview of this process. Chapter 3, "Fastwriting," provides three alternate techniques that will quickly get words and ideas down on paper and will prevent writer's block. Chapter 4 is devoted to yet another fastwriting technique called "Freespeaking" which I have recently developed. It provides a logical bridge between writing and speaking, taking the writer's natural ability to verbalize ideas and quickly translate the verbalized words into written words. The final chapter in this section, Chapter 5, offers revision techniques and also covers organizational methods. Overall, this section will help writers develop a quick draft with fastwriting techniques, then show them how to revise that draft for a critical reader.

Section Two, entitled **SPEAKING,** teaches law enforcement officers how to develop and deliver a speech. Chapter 6, "Informing," outlines the basic techniques for developing a speech to inform. This chapter sets out basic principles of research and organization that can be used in constructing any type of speech. Chapter 7, "Nonverbalizing," discusses in detail a variety of delivery techniques. While the article was written specifically for trainers, its suggested techniques can be used by persons who must deliver a speech, give a briefing, or be interviewed by a panel or promotion board. The article both covers the major nonverbal techniques of delivery and provides clear information on the dynamics of any speech. Chapter 8, "Persuading," is the most academic of all the chapters and the longest. It presents a persuasive speech using the "motivated sequence" format and explains in depth the major theories of persuasion, demonstrating how these theories can be used to persuade an audience to a particular point of view. Chapter 9, "Answering Questions," provides tips on how to answer questions from an audience—a skill vital to any public speaker.

Section Three, **COMMUNICATING IN SPECIAL SITUATIONS,** focuses on a communication situation that is crucial to police work: Chapter 10, "Communicating in a Crisis," provides strategies for public information officers to use when dealing with the news media during a crisis situation.

This book is designed as a companion to supplement *Survival Writing,* published earlier (1986) by Kendall Hunt. With *Survival Communication,* I want both to broaden the scope of how individuals can effectively express their ideas and influence others and to narrow the audience to law enforcement officers. The survival tips in this book will give these individuals the skills they need to convey dynamically law enforcement's message to audiences both inside and outside their organizations. In our information-based society, the work of law enforcement depends on effective communication, and more than ever our officers need sharpened communication skills to accomplish that work. *Survival Communication* aims to give the edge to officers and departments throughout the country.

I
WRITING

Process Writing

2

Many government employees who have just moved up from the "production" or "operations" ranks within their agencies and are suddenly in what are generally called "executive" positions find serious difficulty in writing memoranda, instructions and reports. The strain is aggravated by the fact that the writer knows that not only superiors but also subordinates will be looking over the new executive's first written works to detect and analyze his or her style of communication—that style being expected to also provide clues to overall leadership abilities.

Therefore, a folder of background information may remain on the desk for days or even weeks waiting to be incorporated into a single document. If that type of procrastination happens early on for the new executive it is highly likely it will continue in the months and years ahead, sooner or later producing adverse impact on both performance and career.

In some instances it is a matter of the executive's earlier career being such that almost all effort was concentrated in production or field work which required little or no writing; in other cases it is simply a matter of never having received adequate training in writing skills. Whatever the case, a delay in getting individual writing projects done usually results in the final product being done quickly—just in time to meet the deadline—with the writer knowing that the product was not the best which could have been produced.

The scene is repeated thousands of times daily in government agencies and the private sector around the country. It's not that the executive can't communicate, but sometimes the difficulty in getting started inhibits and frustrates the entire process, making more work than is necessary. The result is a high level of writer frustration and a rushed product that often lacks both the freshness of creativity and the polish of well-revised work.

Reprinted with Permission from *Government Executive Magazine,* February 1985, Title: "Writing—First Hurdle for New Executives."

For the government executive who experiences the problem, a few basic remedies are offered here and, if taken, can help solve the problem and assist with both job performance and career advancement. Those remedies include: a model of writing that is a simple, effective step-like process; strategies for getting things on paper quickly yet effectively to meet deadlines with the best possible final product; and some tips for infusing both creativity and revision into writing.

Analyzing the Task

If most of us were asked to define writing, we would probably mention grammar, punctuation, spelling and a host of other rules that boggle the mind. For the hesitant writer, writing should be recognized as only another form of communication, just like speaking. A typical conversation takes place after we meet another person and a subject is introduced. Our minds switch to an instant search mode, drawing on our experiences, readings and memories to pull back connected bits of information that might apply to the subject. When speaking, we often discover a new approach to the subject, uncovering new ideas as we go. We don't worry about paying strict attention to any rules other than common etiquette, but somehow we manage to articulate our position verbally. Most of the time we are able to convey our messages quite adequately, but if we had to write our responses that would be another story.

However, we have been taught that in order to write we must coordinate and perfectly execute the principles of grammar, spelling, and punctuation while creatively addressing the task at hand, usually with a deadline looming overhead. The results of this juggling act often are hesitation, frustration and procrastination: projects get stalled.

Take a step back for a moment to the time when you learned to write. The concentration in writing was not only on production, but also on editing. With all of the rules swimming around in your head it was no wonder you almost drowned before the pen ever hit the paper. The process of producing an initial draft, while at the same time editing it, halted creativity and gave many of us a stuttering style of writing lacking in fluidity, creativity or personality.

Although any piece of completed writing requires production and careful editing, any writing model which requires both production and editing simultaneously is unproductive and ill-conceived. It is little wonder, therefore, that when we get writing assignments we cringe. It's like asking someone who stutters badly to give a speech to an audience of 500 people. The pressure is on, and many of us have neither the training nor the tools to handle the job.

To survive and advance in any organization, writing is not just helpful, it is critical. In fact, performance standards for many professionals in government now require writing ability as a critical element of the job. The message is clear: writing is basic to our daily survival.

To survive the demands of writing most of us will have to redefine our writing processes and develop a new model. This model should help get us writing more quickly and freely and take us through the entire writing process. It should help produce a final product that is clear, inviting and well-organized and one that conforms to customary standards of grammar, spelling, and punctuation.

The National Writing Project (NWP) was faced with a similar task in 1974. The problem: Students didn't know how to write, and teachers didn't know how to teach the students to write. The failure in the public school systems was so great that nearly 50 percent of the entering freshmen of the University of California at Berkeley were required to take remedial writing during their freshman year. Because of this failure in our schools, the NWP was founded as a possible solution.

Along with others in the profession, the Project has discovered and developed a new model of writing. Now, instead of viewing writing and editing as twin brothers, the Project looks at them as closely related but separate cousins. By separating the two, the Project believes that the flow of writing comes more easily to the writer and that the stuttering effect is reduced to a minimum, if not eliminated. The new writing model is divided into three major components: prewriting, writing, and editing.

Prewriting

In this stage you select an idea or concept that you wish to write about. Allow it to rattle around in your unconscious mind for a minute, an hour or a day depending on your deadline. Your mind will search for any information it may have in memory about this topic. During this step you painlessly begin to connect one idea to another as you discover meaning and direction. You rehearse language in this step, often before the pen hits the paper. Talking to yourself, mumbling and making notes on a piece of scrap paper are symptoms of this stage when it is working well. Ideas may pop into your head as you consciously and unconsciously think about the idea.

This stage may last a few days or a few minutes, depending on how much time you have for the project. You should, however, be aware that allowing your mind the time to play with the idea is a most creative way to get started writing. Neither formal nor structured, this process does not require outlining or anything other than using the conscious and unconscious faculties of your mind.

Writing

Now you begin to put pen to paper. One starting technique is called freewriting. Quite simply, you write about your idea as quickly as you can. The significant difference in this writing model, however, is that you don't worry about punctuation or grammar. Don't even worry about misspellings or the inability to think of the right word; just leave a blank line or a question mark. The faster you write, the more fluid the expression of your ideas and concepts regardless of the organization. What you are looking for is a printout of your ideas to give you a direction and a beginning. You do not want a final copy yet, so don't worry—just write.

To practice freewriting just take out a pen and write a letter to your spouse or friend. Write a note about what you did today. Write as if you were telling a story. As you write you will discover other things to write about, finding your way as you go. That is exactly what freewriting is: discovery. You'll be amazed at what you will learn and how quickly and how well you can write if you're willing to try. Don't be surprised at first if it is a little tough for you to leave a misspelled word or run-on sentence uncorrected. Don't worry, you will get it later. Just write.

The writing will help you discover knowledge deeply imbedded in your mind and reveal its connections to your experiences and readings of years gone by. When you are finished writing, put it down for a day or two if you have time. If not, give it a minute or an hour or whatever you can spare. A time break from your writing gives you some degree of objectivity before you review.

Now you are ready to find which ideas worked for you and which did not. Circle key words or ideas that seem to add to the writing. These will later become focal points for you. This process of review helps lead you to the next step: rewriting.

Rewriting

In this step look at your freewriting and find where the holes are. Some ideas you'll find well developed except for supporting statistics or quotes from authorities to help document your ideas. Other ideas you'll find are only in the formative stage and need heavier research, perhaps a good magazine article or several pages from a specific chapter of a book will flesh it out for you. This step helps point you in the right direction, usually to a library or outside source which may include interviewing someone else in the department more experienced than you on the subject.

When you've filled out some of the areas through additional research (reading and talking), then you're ready to give it another try. Sit down with your research notes spread out in somewhat related piles and freewrite again, connecting new ideas and weaving them into your writing. Write quickly and don't worry about the rules—just get it on the paper. You will be amazed at the fluidity and the speed with which you can write.

Put the draft down for a while again to get some objectivity or distance, and now begin to look at groupings to see where certain ideas fit best. Start moving ideas around. One good system for doing this is to cut up your draft and shuffle the pieces around like cards. Another is to label certain topics with the same letters (A, B, C) to see if you have skipped around in your draft. This will help you to get the same ideas all in one place. Once you have corralled the ideas, rewrite again and continue the process until it fits smoothly. Look for good transitional phrases in your writing to help link the paragraphs together logically and smoothly.

Now you're ready to begin to share your draft with someone else. Developing a person, or better yet a small group of people, who will respond to your writing is essential to any good writer. The group allows you to get outsiders' perspectives and supportive feedback before giving your written work to the final judge, the boss. Developing a community of writers means nothing more than: You read mine and I'll read yours. Make sure that whoever you choose is someone you trust and is positive rather than destructive or the process will not work as well as it can.

After getting your draft back you can try the new corrections or ideas in additional rewrites. Through this rewriting you are continually discovering, adding a little, and taking away anything that does not work. At some point, usually as the deadline nears, you will need to begin final editing which is a line-by-line check for spelling, grammar, usage, clarity, and punctuation. Now, however, you have narrowed down the language and you can perform these tasks as mechanical functions and not part of the creative process.

All the revising may sound cumbersome, but it is done so quickly that it becomes as simple as writing a letter to your best friend. Since it is nonjudgmental, you don't have to worry about grammar or spelling and it is faster than you could ever imagine.

Writing quickly is something that will easily be developed with a minimum of practice. Here are just a few tips:

- Write letters frequently. This style is just like freewriting. It gives you a lot of practice writing, and you will be amazed at how your friends will respond.
- When you have to write something official, try the first draft like a letter to a person, "Dear Joe, . . ." Write it just as you would write a letter or as you would tell a friend. Remember to keep editing (grammar, punctuation, spelling) out of the initial drafts.
- Give yourself some objectivity between drafts. Put it down for a while, then go back and review it.
- Develop a cadre of friends with whom to share writing. Don't do it alone. It is not as much fun, and you will miss a lot of good outside ideas that will add a lot.
- Trust your mind to do a good internal scan search. You'll be surprised at what you know when you start to put your ideas on paper.
- The earlier you get your ideas on paper, the quicker you begin to dissipate the anxiety associated with writing.

Law enforcement officers are trained to shoot for survival to get ready for the event they hope never comes—a gunfight. Fortunately, for many, it never does, but they train regularly just in case. Most officers and other government executives, however, never train to write for survival even though they know it will be critical not once, but hundreds and thousands of times as they try to advance within their organizations.

If you regard writing as a process and not an event, you'll be able to quickly get projects started, meet deadlines, write creatively and survive any assignment.

Fastwriting

3

Not too long ago Jack Nicholson starred in a movie called *The Shining* in which he played a writer trying to finish a book. To get some solitude, he took a job as a resort caretaker. He brought his family to the resort, which was deserted for the winter, and began writing his book. Suffering severely from writer's block, he crumpled up reams of paper and threw them into the wastebasket. Finally, he resorted to re-typing the same lines over and over again, becoming more and more psychotic as he did. Eventually he went mad and tried to kill his family. Now *that's* writer's block!

We've all suffered from writer's block—that screeching of the pen to a halt on a piece of paper—hopefully, however, not to the extent that Nicholson did in *The Shining*. Unfortunately, writer's block usually comes at the most inopportune moments, like the night before a report is due. Writer's block is a manifestation of writing anxiety that many people suffer from, and much research has been done on the concept of writing anxiety.

While numerous reasons have been offered to describe why people have writer's block, one reason seems to be that people can't quickly get their ideas on a piece of paper. Instead, they are constrained by previous myths about perfection, myths about what a writer is, and myths about their own writing abilities or inabilities—all of which have been ingrained since early school days. However, several fastwriting techniques allow blocked writers to get ideas and words on a piece of paper quickly. Further, such early writing can alleviate the added anxiety that a looming piece of writing has on any author. This chapter will outline three fastwriting techniques which can help writers relieve their anxiety by producing initial drafts quickly and painlessly. These techniques are freewriting, brainstorming, and webbing.

Theoretical Background

Before delving into each one of these techniques, I need to explain theoretically why it appears that one or all of these techniques might appeal to people—to all people. First, let's look at the brain's structure to see how these techniques may take advantage of that structure.

13

First of all, the brain is a two-lobed (hemisphered) organ—the right brain controls the left part of the body and the left brain controls the right part of the body. Through research and brain surgery conducted on epileptics, scientists have discovered that the brain has two hemispheres which are differentiated extensively and have certain functions associated with each of them.

The brain acts like two computers in tandem. The right brain controls such things as holistic thinking, spatial relations, art, and sex: an analog computer. The left brain, on the other hand, concerns itself with logic, analysis, math, and science: a digital computer. These two hemispheres—two computers—talk to each other constantly through a bundle of nerve fibers called the corpus callosum which acts like a coaxial cable joining two computers. It is through this communication between the two hemispheres that human beings can function in an integrated way: being able to walk and chew gum at the same time.

While both brains communicate continually, each of us has a preference on which side of the brain we prefer to work. To determine which side you prefer, ask yourself whether or not you prefer analysis to holistic thinking; math to humanities; and working with outlines to wildly producing ideas and organizing later. If you answered yes to each of these, then you likely have a preference for using the left brain. On the other hand, if you answered no to each of these, the chances are likely that you prefer right-brain use. Scientists and mathematicians usually have a left-brain preference, and most people who like the humanities—History and English—tend to be right-brain dominant. Although there are few conclusive judgments, brain hemisphericity does give you some perspectives on how people think.

How do fastwriting techniques fit into all of this? Quite simply, the three fastwriting techniques appeal to various parts of the brain or individual hemispheres.

Freewriting

First, let's talk about freewriting. To freewrite, all you need to do is sit down and pick a topic. Select a comfortable seat, a favorite pen, and a preferred medium on which to write. Each of these factors (and others) affect our writing comfort. Next, write about the topic as if you were writing a letter to a friend—someone who you trust; someone who knows perhaps that you don't know how to spell every word in the English language; and someone who knows you've got trouble with commas. Most importantly, choose your fictitious audience based upon someone who won't laugh at your ideas. Freewriting is nonjudgmental. It's quick, easy, and highly idea-centered. "Idea-centered" means that the sole purpose of freewriting is to get as many of your ideas on paper as quickly as possible. Thus, freewriting focuses clearly on ideas, not language correctness. In fact, it's the obsession for precise language which initially causes writer's block for many people. To freewrite, you need only follow a few simple instructions. First, write for a steady period of time, 10–15 minutes, but not much more than 20 minutes because it's a very intense process and can become tiring. In that period of time you can produce several pages of writing and at least have a foundation for future drafts—a place to begin construction. You'll have captured some ideas in words which you can begin to organize in the revision process. Freewriting appeals to both right- and left-brain people, with a slight preference for right-brain people because of its flow and idea-centeredness, or so it appears from my experience. However, it's worthy to note that writing and language are controlled by the left brain.

Brainstorming

Second, I'd like to suggest brainstorming, or as its called by some, freelisting; a favorite technique used in business and industry. This technique simply requires the writer to sit down with a piece of paper, a pen, and an open mind. Instead of writing in sentences, as in freewriting, you merely list your ideas as fast as you can. Take that initial list of ideas and begin to break it down into its component ideas: sublists. Then break down the components until you have broken down a particular idea as far as you can. By continuing to make lists and lists of lists, you're forcing yourself to analyze an idea and break it down into its component parts. In minutes this technique provides you with a basic outline of components with each major idea broken down into subheadings and each subheading broken down into sub-subheadings. Eventually you can quickly and easily produce an outline from such a listing. Again, the advantage of brainstorming or freelisting is that it's both fast and nonjudgmental and therefore idea-centered. When brainstorming, it takes no more than 15 or 20 minutes to outline any short topic. The only rules are that it be done quickly and that you suspend any personal judgment (i.e., you don't laugh at any of your ideas). After you finish, put the list down and turn to it later to begin pruning. This particular process appeals very strongly to left-brain people because it's so analytical. Left-brain people love lists and outlines, and brainstorming fills the bill.

Webbing

A third fastwriting technique, webbing, allows you to "see what you're writing." Webbing can be done quickly and is an artistic and spatial method of planning a piece of writing. You merely place the idea in the center of the page in a large circle and then draw lines off of that to other smaller circles that will contain sub-ideas. Then break those sub-ideas further into their smaller components. After 20 minutes of webbing, a picture will appear, giving you a global concept (right brain) of your writing.

Writers who use this technique can have a quick picture or diagram of what their writing looks like. This picture serves as a road map for future revisions because it allows the writer to begin the writing process. Again, this is a nonjudgmental technique that should be done quickly. Use a large piece of paper so that you can spread out. Sometimes different colored pens will help differentiate ideas for you. After you complete the process, it's useful to sit down with others and go through it again, adding the richness and variety of others' ideas as well.

Each one of these techniques has a special appeal to certain people. No technique is necessarily better than the others, but they all offer a place from which to start. They can free up ideas and get them on a piece of paper quickly so that revision can begin, for no revision can begin until we have some raw material to work with. Often, mining out the raw material is what causes writers great anxiety. To relieve this anxiety, there are three techniques to use: freewriting, brainstorming or freelisting, and webbing. Test these ideas out as others have and discover their power.

Freespeaking

4

Few of us shy away from a conversation with a friend or refuse a phone call from a coworker on account of poor verbal language skills. Because we've learned the skill of speech at birth and we practice constantly, it holds no fear for us.

Writing, however, gets quite a different response. Most of us avoid it at all costs. Remember the first committee meeting you ever attended? How many people volunteered to write up the report? Writing has truly become an aversion of our times, and those who must write usually regard the task as unpleasant and difficult.

But the toughest part of writing is just like the toughest part of jogging or dieting: getting started. Overcoming inertia is always more difficult than keeping the ball rolling. If you could begin writing quickly—get that start *before* you have time to think how much you don't want to do it—you'd reduce most of the anxiety attached to writing.

Admit it. Most of us prefer speech to writing. Speech is quick and reliable, and since we practice it daily, we feel more proficient at it and confident with it. Then why not lead with your strong suit—speech?

Among the great protections provided by the U.S. Constitution is Freedom of Speech. In America we all cherish this right and, no doubt, it was among the first freedoms set forth in the Bill of Rights because of its importance to a free country. May I then suggest that you exercise this right and join the ranks of those who practice "freespeaking."

What exactly is freespeaking? It's a simple technique to get a written draft quickly and easily on paper—recorded brainstorming. You merely talk with or lecture to an imaginary audience: your reader(s). One hint to keep in mind when you begin is to suspend all judgment as you freespeak. Freespeaking, when done correctly, mimics talking to yourself or to someone else. Haven't you ever told off your boss, a

Reviewed by *Training Magazine,* March 1986, Title: "How to Talk Yourself into Writing."

bill collector, or that nosy neighbor while riding down the highway? If you've ever found yourself rehearsing a speech out loud to hear what you'll sound like or even explaining a problem of yours to a trusted friend on the phone, you've been practicing freespeaking.

When writing we seek instant perfection, but early in the writing process perfection can inhibit fluency and thus our ability to produce a working draft quickly. But, when speaking, we're much less critical and a lot more freewheeling which makes our speech more fluent than our writing. So, forget the burden of perfection that writing a draft may pose and use freespeech to keep your writing flowing. For example, if you say something to an audience you don't think is correct, you don't stop and start all over again. You just put it another way by saying "in other words" or a similar phrase which keeps normal speech flowing with little interruption. Freespeaking keeps your draft flowing as though you were engaged in a conversation completely void of any perfection baggage.

Freespeaking thus allows you to get those ideas out of your head and onto paper as quickly and painlessly as explaining them to someone. When freespeaking, record your words using a tape recorder. Recording enables you to reduce your conversation and ideas to a written document which you can edit and rewrite.

One similar-looking but distinctly different form of this technique—dictation—has been around for years. Dictation, however, is just that: Dictation with a capital "D." The word *dictation* posits a dictator—one person talking into a dictaphone. And because dictators often forget the audience, they forge blindly ahead without ever considering the needs of that audience. Read a typical piece of dictated writing and you'll see pompous, convoluted, wordy language that is guaranteed to leave the reader cold.

Freespeaking avoids the pitfalls of dictation. Because freespeaking isn't usually structured (how often do you speak to a friend or yourself and say "paragraph" or "period?"), you're never tempted to treat the initial freespoken draft as a final one—it *looks* like an initial draft. But dictation, with the addition of paragraphs, often looks physically attractive enough to send out. We reread it but the mentality seems to be that since it looks attractive enough and says generally what we want, to heck with it, let's sign it out—after all, it *looks* good. What we often end up signing out might look good at first glance but could be awful after a second reading. With freespeaking you're not at all tempted by the illusion of completion.

Freespeaking is a process, not an event. It requires the writer to follow several simple rules to ensure a creative product that is produced with a minimum of anxiety. These rules are:

1. Think about what you want to say.
2. Imagine your audience seated before you.
3. Don't edit as you speak.
4. Remember: Freespeaking is only the first part of the process.
5. Freespeak again if necessary.
6. Put away the draft a while for objectivity.
7. Prune back what doesn't work—even if you like it.
8. Share your drafts with someone else.
9. Rewrite as many times as necessary.
10. Edit your work.

This article will explain each freespeaking rule and take you through the process. You'll find the process simple, direct, and effective. More importantly, within minutes of reading it, you'll be able to start that draft you've been avoiding for weeks.

These are some simple freespeaking rules for successful writing:

Prespeaking

Rule #1: *Think about what you want to say.*

Before you write on any topic, take time to think. Like a computer which stores bits and bytes of information, your mind also salted facts away in its unconscious for years. We've all heard the old saw: "I need time to sleep on it." This saying summarizes the best advice a writer can get. Giving your brain time to access its storage of information—sleeping on it or thinking about it—is much like running a random search on a computer. If you allow time, useful connections will emerge.

Sometimes—when the boss wants it now—you'll have only a minute to get your thoughts down, but most often you'll have hours, even days before the writing is due. When you do have time, allow time to sleep on it.

To further stimulate thought, write the idea or project name on an index card and put it in the center of your desk, on the dashboard of your car, or on the top of your dresser. Put it wherever you spend time. You'll be surprised how much subconscious stimulation your mind will get from such a simple activity. Thoughts will begin to simmer, bubble and boil over. When this happens the urge to write or speak gets powerful. You'll even find yourself mumbling—a telltale sign you're ready for freespeaking.

Rule #2: *Imagine your audience seated before you.*

A primary advantage of freespeaking is that it forces you to address a particular audience. First, decide to whom you are speaking. Narrow it down to a friend or a particular group if you like, but the more narrowly you focus, the more clearly you will speak and, eventually, write. Imagine the audience sitting before you—see the faces, the postures, the nonverbal expressions. In short, imagine individual people, not an abstract entity, right there conversing with you.

What kind of language would this particular audience like? Is it (the audience): formal or informal? friendly or restrained or even hostile? high-flown or down-to-earth? from Texas or Boston? interested in the topic or merely tolerant of it? young or old? Let your imagination work up a good checklist so that you can determine the kind of words you should use when speaking.

We automatically do this fine-tuned audience analysis when we speak. For example, we might explain something to experts in a field, then turn right around and literally translate it for laymen. In conversation we have learned to make these conversions quickly and naturally. Therefore, if we use the technique of freespeaking in our writing, we will shortcut a lot of the miseries of tone, style, and diction at the outset.

Speaking

Rule #3: *Don't edit as you speak.*

We all have a tendency to try to do things correctly the first time. In writing, however, this practice leads to slow or no-word production and to poor overall conceptualizing because we get hung up on particular parts and lose sight of the whole along the way. Freespeaking gets us away from self-correction and self-doubt and takes us to the initial task at hand: self-brainstorming.

While freespeaking, don't criticize yourself for anything you say, and don't stop and start the tape recorder as you might do with a dictaphone. Remember this is *not* dictation—it is recorded brainstorming. Idea production is the goal, not correct pronunciation, grammar, or punctuation.

Rule #4: *REMEMBER: Freespeaking is only the first part of the writing process.*

Every writer has to begin somewhere and that's the value of freespeaking—it gets you started. Freespeaking also enables you to self-search accurately. You find out through your own language what you know and don't know, and how you feel about the topic—you end up with a point of view or slant from which you can approach your selected subject. While it's fun, fast, and natural, freespeaking only begins the writing process.

Once you've self-searched, look for holes in your argument or approach: what about specific details or narrative illustrations? Once you've found the holes, fill them with hard data. For the information that will give weight to your ideas, interview others who are knowledgeable on the subject and then, if needed, do research at the library.

Respeaking

Rule #5: *Freespeak again if necessary.*

Once you've gathered enough information through investigation of self, others, or libraries, you're ready for another session. If writing slows you down at this stage or if you're an especially verbal person, try respeaking. Like rewriting, it serves to hone your ideas and improve your expression. But here, rather than writing, you take advantage of your natural, strong suit: speaking. Sit down or stand up with your research notes in front of you; review them; then begin to freespeak, connecting new ideas and weaving them into your talk.

Rule #6: *Put away the draft a while for objectivity.*

When you've completed the draft don't rush to redraft it unless you have a time problem. Try to put it down for a while. Time away from anything, especially writing, provides objectivity. Have you ever read a letter you wrote years ago? Or an old high school or college paper? I'm sure you found things you'd change now, but back then you probably thought it was perfect. The more time the better. But don't get carried away—you don't need a month or a year—that's procrastination.

Rule #7: *Prune back what doesn't work—even if you like it.*

When you review your draft, look for emerging themes and ideas. Determine how and where these might be logically linked or grouped to be effective for the reader. Take a pair of scissors to the draft: Cut it up and move segments around to place the ideas in similar groups. Try various transitional words and phrases to help connect the ideas into a logical flow. If you liked cutting and pasting shapes in grammar school, you'll love this part of the process.

As you go through your draft, cutting and pasting, try also to remove language and ideas that don't fit. Freespeaking naturally creates excess verbiage that sounds good while you're speaking but is often irrelevant or redundant when written. Cut out clutter from your draft and save time for the reader. You'll find it especially hard to cut words or phrases you like, but if you're ruthless now you'll save yourself grief later. Chances are very good that someone down the line will cut it anyway.

Rule #8: *Share your drafts with someone else.*

Whether to a person or a group, whether to colleagues at work or friends, you should show your work to others if you want an objective view. Select people you can trust to be honest and supportive—both essential qualities. You need neither misplaced praise from well-meaning friends, nor worthless censor from well-intentioned realists, but rather an encouraging but honest critique of your work. This rule, one of the most important ones, is often ignored.

Rule #9: *Rewrite as many times as necessary.*

Rewrite your draft as often as necessary to get a quality final product. Good writing demands patience. Writing is best done in a series of drafts, and its biggest enemies are the deadline and your own lack of patience. Put away each successive draft for a while. Go back to your draft with a fresh eye and *redraft.*

Rule #10: *Edit your work.*

Through this rewriting you are continually discovering, adding a little, and taking away anything that does not work. At some point, usually as the deadline nears, you will need to begin final editing which is a line-by-line check for spelling, grammar, usage, and language, and you can perform these tasks as mechanical functions, not as part of the creative process.

Conclusion

We all have powerful verbal skills which help us to make it through life each day. To get food, companionship or a promotion, we have to explain what we want. Freespeaking takes advantage of a natural skill we all practice many times a day without even thinking about it. Freespeaking can remove the drudgery of the first draft and give creativity and freedom to our writing process.

Revising 5

"There are only two powers in the world, the sword and the pen; and in the end, the former is always conquered by the latter." Spoken, surprisingly enough, by Napoleon—a military genius who was more comfortable with "the former"—these words express a fact of life that still holds true today: the written word powerfully affects the conduct of the world, even on the most workaday levels. Preliminary investigations to obtain a search warrant, for example, must be written; so too must arrest warrants, wiretap affidavits, case reports, internal memoranda, and interdepartmental letters. Yet while today's law enforcement officers are trained to feel at ease with updated versions of Napoleon's power of the sword, they often are intimidated by demands on their writing skills.

Consider, however, how important these skills are to law enforcement officers. After an investigation is begun, an officer may wait months or even years before presenting his case to the grand jury and testifying in court. What was once a vivid recollection to the officer has become a memory dimmed by time and intervening experiences. What now endures but the report? The countless hours of interviewing, collecting evidence, and following leads have been reduced to a package of papers. The written document is not only the enduring memory of what happened months or years ago, but also the final reference—the evidence, in fact, with the officer's testimony, on which guilty or not guilty rulings will be determined.

Fortunately, the ability to write well is a learned skill—not at all some inborn "gift" that some have and some don't. To write well, one need only understand a few simple rules and enforce them at every writing opportunity.

The following rules go far in covering the territory. If each officer used them as a checklist after writing any document, his or her writing skills—as well as the document itself—would quickly improve.

1. Be concise.
2. Be clear in meaning.

Reprinted with Permission from *The Investigator's Journal* by The National Association of Federal Investigators, Fall, 1986.

3. Avoid specialized jargon.
4. Use proper word order.
5. Organize writing.

Law enforcement writing, above all, must be accurate—accurate in use of quotation, in not omitting important facts, and in not drawing conclusions that are based on assumptions.

General Rules

1. Be Concise

In his essay, "Politics and the English Language," George Orwell wrote, "If it is possible to cut a word out, always cut it out." Cutting out the fat of a sentence not only makes it shorter—and easier to remember—it also makes it easier to understand. As a general rule, sentence length should be kept to 20 words, though varying length is important too.

Another way to keep the number of words down and the understanding level high is to make positive statements instead of negative ones. The following sentences demonstrate this principle:

Negative form: The chief did not think that the report was at all necessary.

Positive form: The chief thought the report unnecessary.

The first sentence contains 12 words, while the second has only six—a 50% reduction. Can you imagine the savings in a department's filing space over several years if all its documents could be cut in half? Consider the reduction of paperwork in departments which generate thousands, if not millions, of pages of copy a year. Clearly the savings can be counted in dollars as well as in space.

In *Elements of Style,* Strunk and White state, "A sentence should contain no unnecessary words, a paragraph no unnecessary sentences, for the same reason that a drawing should have no unnecessary lines and a machine no unnecessary parts."* Just as sentences must be concise, so too must paragraphs. The paragraph, interestingly enough, originated with ancient Greeks and was used as both a resting place and a reference spot for the reader. Conventionally, it should present a single thought; all the sentences within it should relate to and develop

---

*William Strunk, Jr., and E. B. White, *Elements of Style,* 2nd ed., (New York: Macmillan, 1972), p. 14.

that thought. Newspapers may use single-sentence paragraphs to make the pasted-up copy easy to read, but report writers especially should try to compose paragraphs of four or more sentences.

2. Be Clear in Meaning

A transactional writer writes, obviously, to be understood. He must, therefore, strive for clarity in subject and expression. Rudyard Kipling has summed up in verse the components necessary to writing clearly on any subject:

> I keep six honest serving men
> (They taught me all I know)
> Their names are What and Why and When
> And How and Where and Who.

Besides addressing only the essential features of one's topic, one can improve the clarity of a piece by using concrete words and avoiding abstract ones. The following sentences are examples:

Abstract usage: The robber held a gun.

Concrete usage: The robber pointed his revolver.

After reading the first sentence, the reader doesn't know whether the robber had an automatic pistol or a revolver, whether he was holding it by the barrel, cradling it in his arms, or carrying it around in a paper bag. By contrast, the second sentence is clear and precise; it lets the reader *see* what happened.

Clarity can be improved by striking all instances of wordiness and redundancy. Writers should avoid phrases like "ask the question" when the word "ask" will work; they should scratch "assembled together" when "assembled" fills the bill. Our language is full of doublets and phrases that can be expressed in one word. While these phrases sound colorful when spoken, they are often empty of meaning when written and serve only to confuse.

3. Avoid Specialized Jargon

Writers must take care to avoid the use of "jargon"—that is, the specialized language of their particular group. Computer people, scientists, businessmen, and law enforcement officers all have their own specialized vocabularies that may be explicable within their own circle but sound like Greek to the layman. Since many law enforcement communications are eventually made available to the general public, writers must be careful not to use terms that the public won't understand.

Jargon:	The bluecoat put the robber in irons.
Clarified:	The policeman arrested and handcuffed the robber.

4. Use Proper Word Order

To be understood easily, a writer must carefully order the words in each sentence. He or she should try to write direct, active sentences where the subject of the sentence performs the action.

Active Voice:	The robber stole the money.

Indirect, passive sentences, of course, are very fashionable in officialese, but their overuse, in fact, has almost singlehandedly caused the outcry for better writing.

Passive Voice:	The money was stolen by the robber.

Here the subject (money) is acted upon (was stolen), and one is struck with an awkward prepositional phrase to house the real actor of the piece (robber). Often writers will drop the awkward phrase, thereby eliminating the sentence's most critical piece of information:

Active:	Patrolman Smith shot the burglar.
Passive:	The burglar was shot.

The effect of the passive voice is generally to soften the directness and clarity of the idea and to lengthen the prose—exactly the opposite of what the writer wishes to do.

The word order of modifiers in a sentence can also clarify or confuse. Many jokes, in fact, rely on poor ordering for their humor; one need only consider the song, "Throw Mama from the Train a Kiss." As a general rule in writing, modifiers should be close to the words that they modify: the greater the distance from the word modified, the greater the degree of ambiguity and confusion. An example of this is:

Confusing:	The detective noticed a large stain in the rug that was right in the center.
Clear:	The detective noticed a stain in the center of the rug.

5. Organize Writing

Just as word order logically (one hopes) organizes the sentence, so the ordering of ideas—in paragraphs—logically organizes the whole composition. Material must be organized logically or the reader will be unable to follow the text and so will not understand the point of your writing.

Organization is the structure that holds the substance of any letter or report together; it is the backbone that supports the words, sentences, and paragraphs. As a general rule, writers should begin a report with a paragraph that tells the main ideas of the document in the order they will be discussed. The following is an example of a simple report detailing the information and the body.

Introduction: During the morning of January 30, 1986, three men broke into a private home on South Street and Vine, carrying away jewelry, silver, and electronic equipment. At 1:00 P.M., Officer Smith found three men wearing diamond earrings that matched descriptions of the stolen goods, and he arrested the men as suspects. At 4:00 P.M. they were released on bail pending further investigation.

Body of Paper: 1. Detailed facts of the burglary, including descriptions of stolen goods.
2. Detailed descriptions of the suspects and the circumstances of their arrest.
3. Details of the investigation thus far.

The conclusion of the document, of course, must sum up the results and indicate the necessary follow-up action.

Depending on the subject of the document, the writer can choose different strategies of organization. To describe events, as in the above example, he or she would logically use chronological ordering, starting with the earliest event and proceeding chronologically to the last event in the sequence.

If, however, the writer is attempting to explain an idea or convince others to accept a proposal, he or she might begin with specific details the reader will accept, then generalize from them until the reader finds himself agreeing with the writer's overall idea. Using this strategy a writer might propose:

Introduction: Because our uniformed police have inadvertently been hassling undercover agents, I propose these agents wear baseball caps with orange stripes as covert identification badges.

The body of the report will then detail specifically all the "hassling" incidents to date, with their real and potentially harmful results, so that by the end the reader will be anxious to agree with the writer's conclusion that baseball caps should be issued to all undercover agents as a safety measure.

A third organizing strategy reverses the specific-to-general order. The writer can lead the reader through a series of *general* truths, then conclude with a *specific* application he or she wants accomplished. Consider the following argument from general principles to specific action that a police writer could propose to the community:

- You tell me you don't want your house robbed.
- You will agree the police can't assign officers to individual houses as a regular duty.
- You will agree that police patrols can only deter, not prevent robberies.
- You will agree that private citizens have civic responsibilities.
- You will agree that alert neighbors might spot suspicious activity on your property, as you might spot the same on theirs.
  Therefore
- Why don't you help organize a Neighborhood Watch Organization?

Special Problems in Police Writing

Quotes

The use of direct quotations in reports is critical because so much of policework deals with recording what others have said. In court the officer must swear under oath that an individual said exactly what that officer recorded in his report. Faltering on the stand over the accuracy of a direct quote will weaken the credibility of the officer's testimony. Therefore, when an officer is reporting a conversation and is unsure of the precise words used, he should simply *indirectly* quote the individual. The following is an example:

Direct Quote: The woman said, "Help me! Someone has hit me and taken my purse."

Indirect Quote: The woman said that she called for help because someone hit her and then took her purse.

Errors of Omission

An error of omission can be as damaging as an error of commission. Police reports sometimes suggest in the wording that improper procedures have been followed when, in fact, the procedures were impeccably followed. Nevertheless, the defense in any legal action will seize on the suggestion and use the actual text of the police report for its own purposes. Reports, therefore, should be accurate, complete, and should always include a statement that proper police procedures were followed.

| Omission: | "Mr. Jones was caught, interrogated, and he confessed." |

This sentence fails to note that the police warned the subject of his rights under the Miranda Act. This omission is a significant one that would make any defense attorney's day. The revised sentence should read:

| Corrected: | "Policemen arrested the man and read him the Miranda rights. After he waived these rights in writing, he was interrogated and he confessed." |

Conclusions Based on Assumptions

Police writers must always review their reports to doublecheck that they have not drawn conclusions based on personal assumptions. Conclusions based on scientific or factual data, of course, are both proper and necessary, but those based on the writer's personal opinions are not. Rather than writing, "The subject was crazy," the writer might state with perfect accuracy, "The subject spoke in disconnected sentences and walked into the wall."

Conclusion

Policemen are expected not only to protect citizens from crime, but also to document their observations and actions on paper. Because truth and justice often depend on the clarity and accuracy of police writing, law enforcement officers should be as well trained in writing as they are in investigating and enforcing the law. Writing to be understood— and especially writing so as not to be misunderstood—is a goal every officer can achieve with a minimum of effort: he or she need only concentrate on writing clearly and briefly and on checking work for accuracy of statement. Observing the rules outlined in this article may not make the police officer the next Pulitzer Prize winner, but such a practice will certainly make that next report more readable and that next testimony more accurate.

II
SPEAKING

Informing

6

A professional golfer always makes a booming tee shot look so easy. He approaches the tee with a look of confidence, and after a couple of practice swings, pulls the club back smoothly and smacks the ball straight down the fairway. What we never see, however, are the hours of practice or the constant fine tuning of shots on the driving range that helped engineer that effortless drive. Experienced public speakers also appear relaxed, even casual, in their deliveries. But rest assured, the key to good public speaking is the same as the key to good golfing—preparation.

Preparing a Speech

The speech to inform is composed of three major sections—the introduction, the body, and the conclusion. The introduction engages the audience with an attention getter, makes them want to know more, states a thesis that gives direction to the speech, and provides an initial presummary of the major supporting points of the speech. The body provides evidence establishing the credibility of the main supporting points and the main thrust of the speech. The conclusion provides an overall summary of the speech by restating the thesis and main points and ends with a final statement that provides the speech with a sense of completeness and gives the audience a sense of finality.

Choosing a Topic

The request for a speech usually comes by letter or a phone call: "Could you talk to our club about law enforcement?" The topic is most often left to the speaker's discretion. How should you choose a topic that will be suitable for a particular group? The answer is simple: Let the topic choose you. Why hunt for a topic that sounds impressive but may not be in your area of expertise or is of little interest to you? Let

Reprinted with Permission from the *FBI Law Enforcement Bulletin,* September 1985, Title: "How to Prepare an Informative Speech."

something that interests you become something that you use to interest others. You will be amazed how easily you can prepare a speech on an exciting subject and how the audience will catch your enthusiasm.

For example, if your speciality is juvenile crime and you've been asked to speak to a group of businessmen, why not stick to your strong suit (juvenile crime), while suitably tailoring your speech to the needs and interests of businessmen—profit and loss. The topic of teenage shoplifting might also be a good one for you.

Next, consider your audience. What is their educational background? How old are they? What is their socio-economic level? How large is the audience? Match the topic with the audience. Don't speak to senior citizens about how to protect their businesses from fraud when most of them are retired. More interesting to them would be a speech on scams and bunco schemes of which they might be targets.

To help you analyze the group, try to meet with the person who asked you to speak and interview him in depth. Ask about the topics other speakers have presented to the group. Determine which speakers have been successful and why. Get some sense of the meeting agenda and what the group expects, versus what they say they want. For example, you may have been asked to give a half-hour speech when, in reality, the meeting schedule allows only 10 minutes. Determine exactly what the group wants before you expend unnecessary energy in the wrong direction.

RESEARCHING THE TOPIC

Interviewing Yourself

After choosing a topic and analyzing the audience, how do you proceed? First, consider your personal experiences. Speaking about your personal experiences builds your credibility because the audience begins to view you as an expert. However, you are at just the first step in the research process.

Interviewing Your Colleagues

The next step is to obtain from your colleagues pertinent information, ideas, and illustrations. Interview them in depth to ascertain what resources they have used when preparing presentations, what cases they have investigated, and what anecdotes or examples they may have that could pertain to your speech.

Going to the Library

Finally, you may want to go to a library to gather some up-to-date statistics and facts that will document your subject and reinforce your thesis. The Criminal Justice Periodical Index[1] and the Reader's Guide to Periodical Literature[2] are helpful references. The Criminal Justice Periodical Index is a particularly good source for law enforcement officers. Published annually, it indexes thousands of articles from major law enforcement magazines by subject, author, and title. The Reader's Guide to Periodical Literature, which indexes popular magazines like Newsweek, Time, and U.S. News and World Report, is excellent for current information about cases and world news.

While periodical guides will direct you to up-to-the-minute events, library card catalogs will guide you to books that may provide background for your topic. Entries are listed by author, title, and subject— three different ways to get the same information. When you find a book, check the table of contents and index first to see if and how the book will help you. You need not read an entire book when a chapter or a few pages will do. For example, if you're researching juvenile shoplifting, refer to a book on juvenile crime, and check both the table of contents and index for those chapters or pages devoted to shoplifting.

Newspapers such as *The New York Times, The Washington Post,* and *The Los Angeles Times* index daily events, providing the wealth of detail on which magazines and books draw. These guides are published monthly and are hardbound annually. You might also try Newsbank,[3] which chronicles over 150 newspapers, using a microfiche system. If your local newspaper is indexed, it could provide you with local examples that would make your speech even more specific and relevant to your audience.

Developing a Thesis

Once you have chosen your topic, develop a clear thesis statement. A good thesis statement indicates to the audience your particular focus, and it helps you organize your speech. It is generally stated in a declarative sentence.[4] For example, while the main topic may be shoplifting, you need to narrow this topic into a statement that will give the speech direction. A suitable thesis statement might be, "Teenage shoplifting has devastating effects on the profit margins of small businesses." Notice how this single sentence both narrows the topic and defines the direction the speech will take. Listeners will automatically anticipate certain kinds of supporting information. What are some of the methods of shoplifting? How much money does it cost? And how do you prevent the loss? Your audience is programmed from the beginning by the thesis.

A poorly constructed thesis statement can cause problems. Many people know that the thesis controls and directs the speech; however, when they apply the concept, the statements produced often neither control nor give any direction. They can be too broad, purely factual, or irrelevant.

The most common error is the overly broad thesis. The speaker often chooses a topic but never clarifies it for the audience. For example, if the speaker merely tells his audience that juveniles will be discussed in the speech, the audience doesn't know what to expect, and often, neither does the speaker. The speaker should narrow the focus of audience attention.

A thesis should not merely be a fact statement. Far more, the thesis must take a stance—establish a focus on the topic. Consider the following thesis: Juvenile crime is a problem. How much of a stance does this thesis take? Will the audience have a clear idea of where the speaker is headed? Is it a narrow enough topic to work with adequately in a speech?[5]

Speakers will sometimes deliver what sounds like a thesis statement early in the speech and then proceed to talk about something totally different, causing either the thesis or the body of the speech to become irrelevant. As an example, the speaker might provide a thesis like: "Juvenile crime can significantly erode profits." Though still somewhat broad, this thesis could work. Suppose, however, that the speaker begins to talk about how slow the courts are to punish or how reluctant juries are to convict juveniles. The audience becomes confused, inattentive, and apathetic.

STRUCTURE

Introduction

Speeches that capture and hold an audience's interest begin with a good introduction. Audiences best remember introductions and conclusions. The purpose of the introduction is to introduce both the subject and the speaker to the audience, to grab the audience's attention, and to create a need in the audience to know more.[6]

The "Grabber"

An effective "grabber" attracts the audience's interest quickly. Grabbers vary widely and are limited only by your imagination.

Everyone loves a story. Any kind of narration immediately creates listeners. Why not, then, consider using one in a speech? When somebody says to you, "I want to tell you a story," you generally move closer or lean toward the speaker. A story grabber will get the attention of your audience naturally, effortlessly, and, at the same time, allow you to relax. You can use conversational, nontechnical language, dissipate excess energies and stage fright, and experience immediate reinforcement as the audience lends its collective ear with interest.

Consider using storyteller techniques to improve your delivery. Keep your eyes on the audience at all times. Eye contact makes the story seem more real, sincere, and natural. Tell a story that illustrates or has a logical link to your topic. If the story does not relate to your topic, your audience will be unable to bridge the gap and will be left thinking about the story while you plunge on alone into your subject.

A second method to use when opening a speech is that of quotes. To be effective, the quote must relate directly to your topic and be from a credible source. If your topic is juvenile delinquency and you quote an expert in marriage counseling, the quote, even if it is relevant, doesn't have as much impact as one from a director of a juvenile delinquency center.

A third way to open your speech effectively is to use a startling statistic. Statistics can be riveting if they relate to your topic, come from a credible source, and create a "wow" response. Once you have found a statistic or two that will impress your audience, be careful not to give in to the temptation of overusing statistics.

Involving the members of your audience by placing them directly into a hypothetical situation is also an excellent way to begin a speech. Like role playing, hypothetical involvement forces listeners to experience vicariously whatever the speaker wishes. Such an opening might go like this: "Consider yourself as a small businessman in inflationary times—not hard to imagine—and day after day you see your inventory shrink as hoards of high school students cruise through your stationery story."

Jokes, favored by many speakers, immediately relax the audience, and in turn relax the speaker who perceives audience laughter as positive reinforcement. Jokes are only effective, however, if they are relevant to the topic and if they are very funny. Nothing is more elevating than a joke that works, and nothing more depressing for a speaker than a joke that fails. Faced with a sober audience after the punchline, most speakers lose self-confidence. If you decide to use a joke, test it first in social settings and be sure that it gets a hearty laugh every time. Rehearse the timing and delivery of your joke, even at the expense of your family and friends.

The purpose of these speech openers, of course, is to rivet the attention of the audience quickly to the speech. Audiences, in fact, decide early in the speech whether they want to listen to it and whether they like the speaker.

Keeping the Audience's Attention

Once you have introduced yourself and your speech topic, you must create the audience's need to know.[7] To do this, you may decide to appeal to the audience's basic needs. When you address the impact of shoplifting on business survival, you may want to appeal to the security needs of your audience. Indicate that the security of the employees and proprietor may be at risk, physically and financially, and that business success may erode as shoplifting reduces the profits. A good speaker must consider the audience's basic motivations to establish a clear need for the speech. Retired senior citizens may have little interest in institutional white-collar crime, but will appreciate a speech on how to defend against white-collar schemes and swindles that affect them personally.

Presenting the Thesis

Now that your audience wants to hear your speech, state your thesis in bold unmistakable terms. Remember, it must comment on or judge the topic and be stated in a single sentence. By limiting and controlling the size of your topic, you will give your speech clarity and direction.

Your thesis for the juvenile delinquency speech to local businessmen might eventually evolve to: "I contend that a large portion of the economic dollar in local business is lost through juvenile crimes because of improper methods for detection and protection." The audience now knows your stand and is programmed to expect supporting evidence and appropriate recommendations.

Presummary

After stating your thesis, briefly outline the main points that support your thesis. This presummary makes the transition from the introduction to the body of your speech, and, more importantly, previews the organization of your speech.[8] In the juvenile speech, you might offer as main points to support your thesis the cost to business of juvenile shoplifting, a profile of a typical juvenile shoplifter, some strategies to detect the offenders, and some ways to prevent the problems.

Body

After completing your research and formulating the information into several supporting main points, you must present them to the audience. To be consistent, you'll want to restate each point in the order you promised in the presummary and then undergird each point with a structure of convincing support documentation.

The general types of effective supporting information are similar to the grabbers found in the introduction: Illustrations or stories, quotes or testimony, statistics, and hypothetical situations.[9]

All hard data used in the speech should be subjected to a three-way test before using it to support a main point. The speaker must ask: Is the data relevant, credible, and accurate?

Relevant data

Your information should be relevant both to the main point and to the thesis it supports. If you're discussing white-collar crime, for example, why use bank robbery statistics to help support your position? Also, ensure that any illustrations used relate directly to your audience. When talking to businessmen, use stories about business, not education.

Credibility

The nature of your source colors the data you use. If your source is well-known and reliable, your data will be quickly accepted. Use well-known authors, quote established practitioners, and refer to reputable periodicals to make your points.

Accuracy

Check and doublecheck facts, statistics, and quotes or testimony. Inaccuracies make the audience doubt whether any of your facts were correct.

Organization

The backbone of any structure is the organization. If you expect to keep the readers by your side as you walk them through your speech, you'll have to use some structuring elements to help strengthen the body of your speech.

First, start strong—always lead with your strongest main point. Burying your strongest point in the middle of your speech means you are burying the information you should be highlighting.

Second, enumerate each of the main points so the audience doesn't get lost on the way. Your audience will thank you for it.

Third, provide transitions for listeners, so if you take a sharp turn, they won't turn down the wrong road. Words that show relationship help make it clear for the audience where you are headed by pointing out the relationship between one concept and another. Using words such as "and," "but," "therefore," and "however" can point the way to your audience quickly and efficiently.

When drafting a speech, you should think of your thesis as the roof that covers the entire speech, spanning it and providing the cover of consistency to all below. This roof must be supported by the pillars or main points (which should be limited to three or four) in your speech. To do its supporting job well, each of these pillars must be able to withstand elements of close scrutiny and doubt from the listeners. To help the pillars stand true and strong, each must be made from reliable, strong brick and mortar—facts, illustrations, testimony. These bricks come from the labor of research which forms and hardens these bricks into uncompromising support.

Conclusion

The conclusion serves as a review for the audience. It is your chance to summarize what you told them in the body and fortify the expectations you raised in the introduction.[10] The conclusion is also, however, a safety valve for any speaker.

The first thing you should do in a good conclusion is restate your thesis. Next, review each one of your main supporting points. Depending on audience attention and time, you can review your main points in greater or lesser detail. If you moved quickly through the body of the speech, you may want to take a little extra time here to ensure a detailed review of each of the supporting points. On the other hand, if you've made your point and you find the audience rustling around, or time is getting late, just touch on the main points quickly by listing them and move into your final statement.

The final statement should function much like the grabber. It should be memorized, should be relevant to your topic, and should be delivered to the audience in an emphatic and appropriate manner. When you are finished, there should be no doubt left in the mind of the audience. They should be prepared to applaud or in some way react to your final statement.

Preparing an effective speech is not easy. Contrary to the belief of many, a good speech requires considerable analysis, research, and preparation. Remember, like any professional, whether addressing the ball on the tee or an audience of 50 or 500, there is no substitute for good, solid preparation.

References

1. *The Criminal Justice Periodical Index* is published three times annually. The first two issues are in paperback, and the final cumulative issue is hardbound.
2. *The Reader's Guide to Periodical Literature* is published periodically throughout the year in paperback, and the cumulative annual edition is hardbound.
3. *The Newsbank Index* is published monthly in paperback, and the cumulative annual edition is hardbound.
4. Edward P. J. Corbett, *Classical Rhetoric For The Modern Student* (New York: Oxford University Press, 1965), pp. 36–37.
5. Ibid.
6. Anita Taylor, *Speaking in Public* (Englewood Cliffs, NJ: Prentice-Hall 1979), pp. 149–156.
7. Douglas Ehninger, Bruce E. Gronbeck, and Alan H. Monroe, *Principles of Speech Communication* (Glenview, IL: Scott, Foresman and Company, 1980), p. 219.
8. Ibid, pp. 219–220
9. Bobby R. Patton, Kim Giffin, and Wil A. Linkugel, *Responsible Public Speaking* (Glenview, IL: Scott, Foresman, and Company), pp. 76–93.
10. Leon Eretcher, *How to Speak Like a Pro* (New York: Ballantine Books, 1983), pp. 99–108.

Nonverbalizing

7

Do not let this unsettle you, but every move you make in front of a training room is noticed by your trainees. While you may speak non-stop to your students, your words comprise a mere seven percent of what's communicated.[1] The other 93 percent is nonverbal, determined by your movements, expressions and gestures.

You may never have received instruction in nonverbal communication. Instruction for trainers often dwells on information and equipment. But with thought to nonverbals and some practice, you can use these silent signals to enhance the effectiveness of your presentation.

The Face

From the moment we're born we learn to read facial expressions for emotions—joy, love, anger—and for judgments—approval, disapproval, interest, disinterest. We "read" others consciously, unconsciously and continuously. In the classroom, students read your expressions to determine the meaning and weight of your words. To be effective, punctuate your lessons with expressions that emphasize critical points. This helps students focus properly on information of varied importance. At the same time, carefully read your students' faces to learn how well your message is being received.

While the whole face best expresses the body's emotion, according to research particular facial features express specific emotions.[2] The eyes are perhaps the most revealing. When we meet people and engage them in conversation, we know how well we're being received and whether our messages are getting through by the degree of eye contact. Effective trainers understand this; they gauge the reception of both self and ideas through conscious eye contact. They most likely, during eye contact with students, ask themselves two simple questions: Do I have credibility with these students? and do they understand what I'm saying?

Reprinted with Permission from *The Training and Development Journal,* August 1985, Title: "Notes Are Not Enough."

In his study conducted at the University of Miami, Steve A. Beebe demonstrated the effect of eye contact on listener comprehension and speaker credibility. In the experiment, speakers gave three different speeches to an introductory speech class. In the first speech, the speakers maintained no eye contact; in the second speech, moderate eye contact; and in the third speech, a high level of eye contact. When asked which speeches had more credibility, the students chose the ones in which the speakers maintained moderate or high levels of eye contact. Beebe determined also that eye contact enhances listener comprehension and speaker credibility.

Through extensive studies of the classroom environment, Robert Sommer determined that students in the center of a typical straight-row classroom consistently participated more than those in any other section of the room. Sommer concluded that speakers should shift continually the physical center of the classroom by moving their eyes and, if necessary, their bodies to encourage full audience participation.

Eye contact can be made on a sweeping or individual basis. Continually shifting the center of a room is accomplished with sweeping eye contact. To do this, simply scan the class from side to side and front to back with regularity. Develop a pattern of sweeps, methodically crisscrossing the audience a section at a time. Don't focus extensively on any one area of the room; divide your time equally between sections. Turn your head and shift your eyes naturally and smoothly. Take care not to dart your eyes nervously or jerk your head from side to side.

Sweeping eye contact maintains audience attention, even when you must refer to notes for a scripted or first-time speech. It is effective also when addressing large groups; sweeping eye contact shrinks the distance between you and the audience, maintaining a group feeling with you as the head. As the distance between you and the students increases, your degree of eye contact should increase to make up for the lack of physical closeness.

With smaller groups you can engage in individual eye contact. It is highly effective in communication, for everyone likes to be recognized as an individual; no one wants to be just another body in the crowd. Especially in our world of social security numbers and other impersonal means of identification, people continually seek personal recognition to compensate.

To make individual eye contact with each student, visually engage a student for one or two seconds and then move on to the next. Move systematically through the class, from student to student, a number of times to ensure that individual time is spent with each person.

44

Individual eye contact is effective in many ways. The attention helps each student develop a sense of relationship with you. The students believe you are speaking to them individually, rather than collectively as a class. Because they are personally engaged, they are forced to become partners in the learning process. And because the individual attention also creates a personal sense of importance, students better appreciate their roles in the learning process.

From Adam Kendon's study of how speakers and listeners communicate, we also know that eye contact transmits a request for reaction. Your individual contact signals a silent request for feedback, persuading a student to respond. Individual eye contact keeps students locked onto the lecture. If the contact is systematic, they follow more closely. It's hard to drift off when you know a cold stare may interrupt your daydream.

What is the reciprocal effect of individual eye contact on the trainer? For one thing, trainers receive essential feedback that tells them if their messages are being received. Quizzical looks, smiles, nodding heads, tapping fingers and shuffling feet all are indicators. These cues may prompt you to explain a concept again, use another example or move on to another idea.

Also, a trainer's class performance is improved by individual eye contact and the reinforcement it draws from the students. People prefer speakers who engage them with eye contact. It sparks positive non-verbal feedback from an audience. This feedback builds the trainer's confidence and leads to better performance. Conversely, if an audience loses interest (through lack of eye contact) or becomes alienated, the trainer may lose verbal fluency. If so, his or her performance will suffer.

The Space

The classroom configuration forms an important relationship between the trainer and the students, and that relationship changes as the trainer moves about the room. As trainers close the distance between themselves and students, the classroom climate becomes less sterile, more social, more personal and psychologically more intimate.

Intimate spatial relationships have a positive effect on the training climate of a classroom. Workshop and break-out groups (small working groups of four or five people broken from a larger group for a specific task) allow the trainer to approach students on a much more personal basis. Because of the smaller group sizes and their informality, the trainer can join discussions as a collaborative coach. Addressing individual members on a closer, more personal level cements stronger bonds between trainer and students and enhances learning.

You can use movement to close or open space, depending on the message you want to convey. When you want to emphasize a particular point or convey a feeling of personal warmth, move closer to the class. If, however, time is a factor and you must quickly review critical information, establish a less personal relationship by increasing your distance from the class (12 feet or more between you).

Effective movement involves walking slowly and deliberately, both laterally (right and left) and toward and away from the class. Be sure to keep your eyes on the class while you're moving to avoid looking nervous. Movement attracts attention; our eyes naturally pick up and track anything in motion. That's why we wave a hand to ask questions in class, hail a cab or call a waiter in a restaurant.

Consider changing the classroom focal point on a regular basis to grasp student attention from different learning perspectives. Simply repositioning a flip chart from one side of the room to the other can alter the spatial relationship in the room and heighten student attention. By varying spatial relationships, you easily can change atmosphere and intensity, adjusting them to the particular lesson.

The Gestures

Gestures carry a lot of weight; their impact should not be underestimated. Although people frequently punctuate their daily conversation with natural gestures, the same people in a public speaking situation often avoid gestures or render them unnaturally. Nervous gestures such as shuffling, rustling notes or fidgeting with a microphone cord distract the audience and hurt the presentation. Meaningful gestures, however, which are natural movements of the arms and hands, can paint a picture, condense material or arouse the audience.

When you draw visual pictures with gestures, students can "see" the point more clearly. Gestures can illustrate quickly and graphically how large or small an object is or its size relationship to something else. You can draw a figure, indicate temperature and underline emotion.

Hand and arm gestures work in concert with facial expressions to aid students in interpreting the trainer's meaning. Gestures also arouse students' interest. Just as the face conveys emotion, body gestures transmit enthusiasm. To stimulate student learning, deliberately cultivate combinations of gestures that work. When relating a delicate point, keep hand and arm gestures controlled. But when underscoring a bold point, be vigorous and animated. By keeping your gestures in sync with your other nonverbal actions and with the topic at hand, you'll avoid sending contradictory signals, which serve only to confuse your audience.

For impact and economy, gestures can replace wordy explanations. Demonstrating a complex task with gestures saves valuable lesson time. You'll agree after trying this simple experiment: Write an explanation of how to fold and place a letter in an envelope. When you're finished, see how quickly you can do the same thing with clear, condensed gestures.

There are several techniques for improving gesturing:

1. Videotape your presentation and play it back with the volume turned off. (Be prepared for a shock when you first observe your gestures this way).
2. Ask fellow trainers to critique your gestures. Others can see things you'll overlook.
3. Try to gesture with both arms and hands to embrace as much of the audience as you can. By using both arms and hands, you'll be able, for example, to indicate relationships between two different things.
4. Keep your hands out in front and working for you, not stuffed in your pockets. Don't let your hands shuffle papers or play with distracting objects like paper clips or rubber bands.
5. Hold lecture notes in the nondominant hand (i.e., the left hand if you're righthanded), and keep notes out of sight except when referring to them. This way you will have at least one hand free for vivid gesturing. (Students expect you to need notes, but they'll get distracted if you wave the notes around).
6. Make gestures in proportion to the size of the audience. Just as it would be inappropriate to use huge, sweeping gestures in an intimate social setting, it also would be wrong to use small, refined gestures with an audience of 300. The larger the audience, the more sweeping and rigorous the gestures must be. In a large auditorium, always consider the people in the back straining to hear and "see" what you are saying.
7. Rehearse gestures in front of a full-length mirror to monitor your progress.

The Touch

Some trainers view touching, which is essential to human development, as taboo in the classroom. By doing so they ignore an important tool of support. Shaking someone's hand when meeting, patting a back when complimenting, and grasping a shoulder when criticizing or reassuring are all effective communicators. Other touches are okay as well.

J. P. Bardeen's study confirms the significance of touching and concludes that people may prefer touch to verbal contact. Subjects of his experiment were asked to interact with what they thought were three different people under three separate conditions. The subjects, however, were interacting with the same person each time. The situation included "touch" only (no talking between subject and person, subject blindfolded); "visual" only (no talking, no blindfold on subject, no touching); and "verbal" only (no touching, subject blindfolded). After the experiment the subjects selected the following adjectives to describe the three encounters: touch—trustful, sensitive, natural, warm; visual—artificial, childish, arrogant, comic, cold; and verbal—distant, noncommunicative, artificial, insensitive, formal. When the subjects were asked which of the three persons they might like to interact with in the future, 47 percent selected the person encountered by touch. Another study involving nurses who frequently touched hospital patients revealed that patients felt closer with those nurses. This study underscores how touch helps develop human relationships.[3] The implications for training are clear. Effective trainer-student touch can tighten their bond, stimulate further communication and, hence, facilitate learning.

A few simple actions can get you started on using touch effectively. One is to use break-out groups of four or five students. These will offer you opportunities to get physically close to your students, create opportunities for your students to share more personally, and help you reinforce relationships with an occasional reassuring touch. When possible, shake hands with your students on the first day of class. Take advantage of the chance to make physical contact and to begin building bonds. Lastly, keep the bonds you make with your students alive with frequent, brief, encouraging pats on the back.

The Sound

No one likes to listen to the drone of a monotone speaker. Vocal characteristics—tone, tempo and volume—truly can make or break a presentation.

Tone refers to the changing pitch of your voice. Tone alters the meaning of words through varying inflection and emphasis. Depending on the emotion with which a speaker delivers a word, that speaker may give the word a new, connotative meaning vastly different from its dictionary definition. As an example, consider the word *boy*. When referring to a young male, *boy* is said with little inflection; the meaning relies heavily on the word's primary (dictionary) meaning. When, however, it is pronounced with an exclamatory inflection—"Boy, you won't believe what I just saw!"—the word *boy* can be used with any number of inflections to indicate disgust, joy or defeat.

Tempo is the speed of speech. Most audiences listen comfortably at a rate of one and a half times the normal speaking rate of 125 words per minute. The gap between these two rates can mean problems for both trainer and students. Student minds may wander off naturally waiting for the trainer's voice to catch up. Daydreaming, lack of attention and even class disruption can occur.

Varying the tempo adds significant quality to any presentation. Either speeding up or slowing down at appropriate, natural intervals to emphasize certain points focuses class attention on the message. It helps students easily identify the concepts you consider important. The underlying concept used to make tempo effective is contrast. This contrast between tempos, when done to emphasize concepts, also can enhance the speaker's persuasiveness.[4] When explaining something that requires energy and force, speed up your voice to lead to a natural crescendo. Then follow with a much slower-paced delivery to attract the audience's attention.

Volume is another important characteristic to consider. All of us have suffered through a trainer who provided good information but whose lack of voice quality put the class to sleep. Volume adds a quality to language that not only stimulates attention, but also highlights words and clarifies meanings.

To add energy and dynamics to delivery quality, decide which points need emphasis, and color them with volume contrast. Contrast can be achieved best by alternating volume between high and low ranges—raising and lowering volume. This variation helps the audience know what you consider to be beneficial or important. Continual loud delivery is no better than constant whispering—both are equally distracting to the audience.

Contrasting volume and the other vocal techniques result in greater credibility for the trainer and stimulate an increase in learner retention.[5] Following are some tips for using your voice to your advantage in the classroom:

1. Highlight lesson plans with colored pens to help you determine where to add emphasis with tempo, tone or volume.
2. Rehearse in an empty classroom, placing a tape recorder several rows back to determine how well your voice carries.
3. Practice with an audience. One or more colleagues willing to hear and critique your presentation can provide invaluable feedback on your voice qualities.

Excellent nonverbal communication skills are not a luxury or frill, but a necessity for the trainer. In a world where students are bombarded constantly with information, trainers are forced to compete for their attention. To be successful, the trainer must reach within and pull out the natural aids—expressions, movement, gestures, touch and sound. A well-rehearsed lecture spiced with expressive nonverbals is certain to make for a winning presentation.

References

1. Mehrabian, A., and Wiener, M. (1967). "Decoding on inconsistent communication." *Journal of Personality and Social Psychology,* 109–114.
2. Ekman, P., Friesen, W. V., and Ellsworth, P. (1972). *The face and emotion: Guidelines for research and an integration of findings* (109–119). New York: Pergamon Press.
3. Agulera, D. C. (1967). "Relationships between physical contact and verbal interaction between nurses and patients." *Journal of Psychiatric Nursing,* 5, 5–21.
4. Mehrabian, A., and Williams, M. (1969). "Nonverbal concomitants of perceived and intended persuasiveness." *Journal of Personality and Social Psychology,* 13, 37–58.
5. Woolbert, C. (1920). "The effects of various modes on public reading." *Journal of Applied Psychology,* 4, 162–185.

Persuading

8

Persuasion fuels our everyday lives. We use persuasion on our jobs when we convince the boss to get new equipment, in our social lives when we change the opinions of our peers, and in our personal lives when we motivate our children to do better in school. Persuasion lies at the core of successful law enforcement as well. Consider a detective investigating, interviewing, or interrogating a suspect without the use of persuasion; consider a police chief who lacks persuasive skills attempting to get the town fathers to support his department. Persuasion isn't a luxury anymore in law enforcement; it's a necessity.

To demonstrate how persuasion can work in law enforcement, this article will analyze the persuasive elements of a routine argument. It will focus on a chief of police from a major city attempting to persuade the city council to approve additional funding for new protective vests. Five major theories of persuasion will be used to analyze this scenario: (1) Monroe's Motivated Sequence; (2) The Theory of Rhetoric by Aristotle; (3) The Theory of Cognitive Dissonance by Leon Festinger; (4) Social Judgment by Sherif and Hoveland; and (5) The Yale Theory.

Police Chief's Speech to Persuade

Dressed in his uniform and accompanied by two aides, the Chief of Police delivers a speech to the city council requesting funding for 250 additional protective vests. The Chief's speech opens with a dramatic story about one of his men who was recently shot and killed. The slain officer was not wearing a protective vest because, with the push for new recruits in recent years, the department could not afford enough vests to distribute to all new officers. The Chief tells the city council that within the last three years, four other officers have met the same fate due to the inadequate vest supply. He then states that he fears the voters will hold the members responsible as they are responsible for public safety, including the safety of policemen.

Co-authored with Yvonne J. Rudiger, 1985 University of Virginia Summer Intern at the FBI Academy.

At this point, the Chief outlines a possible solution: raffle off an automobile donated by a local dealership in order to raise the money for the vests. He explains in detail how the raffle will be conducted and then offers some examples from other cities where this type of fund-raiser has been successful. One department, for example, raffled off a one-week vacation to Florida which was donated by a travel agency. The raffle tickets (which were printed free as a donation) were sold by each officer and his family at $2 apiece. In only three weeks the department was able to raise $1,500.

After offering further supporting statistics and examples, the Chief acknowledges possible objections which may be held by the council members, such as the propriety and the cost of such a program. He discusses each potential objection. The Chief then adds a new consideration by mentioning the recent pressure on the council to provide additional funds for rebuilding the prisons and notes the complaints from citizens about the makeshift facility where the inmates are currently being housed. He highlights the fact that the only way to minimize the city's anxiety over the temporary facility is to increase the visibility of the police patrol. However, the Chief states he cannot risk the lives of his men by putting them on the street without proper protection. He adds that new vests would help take the "heat" off the council while, more importantly, insuring the safety of the patrolmen.

The Chief begins to conclude his speech by reviewing the problem, the duty of the council, the solution, and his proposal. Before closing his speech the Chief recollects the story of the policeman being shot and killed and recounts in detail his funeral. He ends with a direct appeal to each of the council members to take the reasonable course and approve the proposal.

Monroe's Motivated Sequence[1]

The Police Chief's speech to persuade demonstrates an organizing principle common to persuasive speeches—Monroe's Motivated Sequence. This organizational pattern is based on human desires which need to be satisfied,[2] ranging from physiological needs such as thirst and hunger to self-actualization needs such as self-fulfillment. The persuasive speaker comes to the podium with his own individual "need"— one which his audience does not necessarily share—and seeks to share this sense of urgency. However, he knows "you cannot cram ideas down people's throats, but must lead their thoughts easily and gradually toward the conclusion you desire."[3] Monroe analyzed the process that humans normally follow to make decisions and established his motivational sequence.

The motivated sequence consists of five steps:

1. Getting attention (Attention Step)
2. Showing the need; Describing the problem (Need Step)
3. Satisfying the need; Presenting the solution (Satisfaction Step)
4. Visualizing the results (Visualization Step)
5. Requesting action or approval (Action Step)

Monroe believed that since the sequence reflects the steps people should follow when systematically thinking their way through problems, its use in arguments should motivate the listeners to accept the speaker's proposition.[4]

Motivated Sequence Application

In the Chief's speech to the city council we can identify each of the five steps. The Chief chose to capture the council's "attention" by relating the tragic story of the slain police officer. The Chief demonstrated the "need" by saying the department could not afford protective vests for every officer, and reinforced the opening story by citing the mortality statistics for the past three years. The Chief noted the cause of the problem—additional officers had been hired since the council last approved a request for additional vests—and personalized the "need" by making the members aware that voters held them responsible for public safety.

Having fulfilled the Need Step, the Chief then moved to the Satisfaction Step, proposing a car raffle to "satisfy" the need for additional funds. Further, he cited a practical example from another department, giving particular attention to the operational details of the event. He then anticipated possible objections (cost and propriety) and addressed them accordingly to discourage additional objections from being raised.

In the Visualization Step, the Chief "visualized" the results of the approved proposal and the unapproved proposal. If approved, the department would reduce citizen pressure on the council to place more men on the street. More importantly, the new vests would help save the lives of police officers. However, more men could not be utilized without having the necessary equipment, i.e., without approval for the raffle.

The Chief now reached the point where he could appeal for action. He first summarized his speech, then directly asked for the council's approval.

The Theory of Rhetoric: Aristotle[5]

Aristotle was an ancient Greek philosopher who discussed the principles of persuasion in his famous *Rhetoric*. According to Aristotle, the three basic elements of persuasion are: ethos, or the credibility of the source; logos, or reason; and pathos, or emotion. He found that audiences judge credibility according to (1) the speaker's good sense, his ability to recognize the truth; (2) his good character, his ability to tell the truth; i.e., the honesty and sincerity of the source; and, (3) his good will, his willingness to keep the audience's best interests at heart. In other words, the power of persuasion is vested in the speaker rather than the receiver of the message.

To persuade through ethos, the speaker must be knowledgeable (credible) and appear to have the audience's best interest in mind (trustworthy).

Logos, which includes appeals to logic and rational proofs, is established by the speaker when he supplies the receiver with a body of knowledge that is substantiated and supported by believable experience. The argument must be logical, concise, and brief, but it must contain adequate details.

Finally, pathos appeals to the emotions, such as love, hate, anger, envy, pride, and fear. Use of pathos can motivate audiences which are neutral on an issue to commit themselves and take action.

Aristotelian Application to Persuasion

In our scenario the Chief enhanced the status (ethos) of his position by wearing his uniform to the meeting and by bringing assistants with him. Already, however, his ethos was firmly grounded on his established reputation.

In his speech, the Chief demonstrated his good will by offering the council the explanation that they could be held responsible by the voters if his plan was not adopted, and displayed his good character by speaking in a straightforward, direct manner to the council. He clearly showed good sense in recognizing and addressing the problem swiftly and accurately. His overall ethos was also enhanced by his delivery, his style, and the status which he gained from the comments themselves—in short, his performance.

The Chief employed pathos in his speech because he wished to provoke in the council an emotional commitment to his problem. Appealing emotionally to his audience in both the opening and closing words, he was, nevertheless, careful not to be too emotional lest he detract from the logic of his arguments.

Appealing to reason, the Chief used statistics, examples, and a clear problem-needs sequence in his delivery. Further, he put his most important facts up front and buried his least supportable facts in the middle, a technique that is highly effective when arguing from logos. His speech was well organized, his style personal and realistic, and his documentation appropriate as well as accurate.

Cognitive Dissonance[6]

The theory of Cognitive Dissonance holds that human beings seek homeostasis; that is, they want to maintain their lives in well-ordered routines and don't want anyone to rock the boat. Accordingly, all humans adopt certain firm attitudes about any given topic—and judge new information to be (1) irrelevant; (2) consonant, in support of the belief already held; or (3) dissonant, in opposition to the belief held. If they judge the information to be dissonant, they feel stressful, and automatically seek a solution to reduce the stress.

What reduction strategies do humans use, then, to achieve an immediate solution to tension? They will:

1. Tolerate the dissonance. They attempt to hold opposing viewpoints about the subject simultaneously and consequently become more anxious.
2. Change one of the dissonant elements. Seeking to uphold or change their belief in the subject, they will add new supporting information by asking other people or by reading books.
3. Distort the information and/or the sources of that information or attack their credibility.
4. Add consonant beliefs to one side of a dissonant relationship. This functions much like rationalization.

How then can this theory address techniques of persuasion? The theory of cognitive dissonance strongly implies that if you create dissonance (a problem) early in a persuasive encounter, you can exploit this dissonance by offering your solution to produce the desired change. First, you must block or cut off the receiver's tendency to distort the information you are presenting by offering repeated examples that support your premise and by establishing the unimpeachable reliability of your source. Second, you must anticipate the receiver's objections and refute them in the persuasive argument.

Cognitive Dissonance Application

In his speech to the city council, the Chief created dissonance early and effectively by suggesting that voters might hold the council members personally accountable for the deaths of the policemen. The council members believed themselves honest, hardworking, trustworthy people, but the Chief disturbed their belief by suggesting they had reneged on their responsibility.

After creating dissonance, the Chief quickly offered a solution, a strategy based on the Cognitive Dissonance theory. When the council members received the dissonant information, they could tolerate the information, change the dissonant elements, distort the source, or add new beliefs. In all likelihood, however, the council would attempt to distort the information about the vests—say, assert that the vests are too expensive—so the Chief cut off their objections by directly addressing the cost figures. Because his solution was reasonable, workable, and well documented, there is a high degree of probability the council will accept the proposal.

Social Judgment Theory: Sherif and Hovland[7]

A particularly powerful persuasion theory, the Social Judgment Theory is based upon psychological verities. We tend to judge nonphysical objects and social stimuli on the basis of anchors we have created in our world-orientation. If you put your right hand on a cold glass of water and put your left on a hot glass of water and then move either hand to a lukewarm glass of water, you would notice a tremendous contrast in relative temperatures. The lukewarm glass would feel much cooler to the left hand and much hotter to the right hand. This particular effect of contrast, produced by a previously established anchor, demonstrates the principle of this theory.

This theory holds that on any given topic we have a preferred position or anchor for the topic. We perceive every social stimuli and physical object in terms of the internal anchor we've established in the past. Further, for any particular topic we tend to accept information and positions that appear close to our anchor (assimilation) and reject information that appears distant from our anchor (contrast).

Assimilation is a psychophysical phenomenon that makes us perceive similar viewpoints as identical viewpoints—or as much closer than they really are. On the other hand, contrast is the phenomenon by which we see information or viewpoints different from our own as being farther away than they really are. Just as these message distortions occur with physical sensations (hot/cold, hard/soft, etc.), they also govern our perceptions of social issues. Such message distortions, assimilation and contrast, tend to increase personal involvement or ego investment in a topic. This involvement of ego investment makes it difficult to change the mind of someone who is committed to an ego invested anchor. When tied to a strong anchor, a ship is more difficult to move. So, the tide of persuasion must move slowly and higher to shift its position even slightly. Persuasion can change a preferred position on a topic, thereby changing the anchor, which is the basis for what is known as "the gradual revision strategy" of this theory—moving the anchor inch by inch, not foot by foot.

Social Judgment Application

The Chief prepared his speech based upon what he perceived as the city council's position on purchasing vests. Obviously, he believed the council couldn't buy new vests because the budget would not allow it. So, instead of trying to get them to move all the way over to his position he offered a compromising solution: The city council should consider approving an option not involving their money but one which still required their approval.

The Chief believed strongly that vests were necessary immediately, and the council should pay for them. The council's view of the vests is anchored in the position that vests may or may not be necessary, but they are not going to pay for them. If the Chief and the council stick to their views anchored at opposite poles, both parties remain in jeopardy. Adhering to the Social Judgment Theory, the Chief chose to offer a compromising view to the council which required that neither party involved had to drastically shift their anchors or previously held views. This theory also maintains that within any anchor or position there is a latitude of rejection, a latitude of acceptance, and a latitude of noncommitment. In most groups, 30% of the people are for something (latitude of acceptance), 40% are noncommitted (latitude of noncommitment), and 30% of the people are against something (latitude of rejection). Using this theory and these general figures (which vary with the subject and audience), the Chief aimed his comments at the 40% in the noncommitted ranks, assuming that 30% may already agree and 30% may never agree. If he could shift the opinions of the 40% noncommitted toward acceptance, then a 70% majority of the council would vote in his favor.

Implications for persuasion are that moderate discrepancies are best. Large changes can only be made through a successive, moderate change of anchors moving the council closer and closer to the Chief's position.

The Yale Theory[8]

The Yale Theory of persuasion evolved in the 1950s and represented a complete shift in focus from the traditional models. Whereas Aristotle conceived of persuasion as the speaker changing the minds of an audience, the Yale Theory conceives of persuasion as the audience learning new information. Information is learned if it is believable and rewarding, not punishing, which constitutes the first tenet of the model. The second tenet is that persuasion is a two-step process:

1. Reception: Receiving and understanding the information
2. Yielding: Accepting the information

The first tenet sounds very close to the old epicurean principle that people seek pleasure and avoid pain, but it goes one step further and says that persuasion is effected through rewards, not punishment. By implication, creating fear—particularly in an individual—to achieve an end is less effective than apportioning positive rewards. The second tenet focuses the speaker's attention directly on the audience to be persuaded. The two-step process which the audience must go through (reception and yielding), can be affected by various characteristics of the audience, i.e., intelligence, self-esteem, involvement, and anxiety level.

For an audience member to understand your ideas, he must have a certain degree of intelligence. Intelligent people might understand quickly what you are saying, however, they might resist accepting the information due to their own counterarguments and so remain unpersuaded. Thus, the more intelligent an audience the less likely that they will yield to persuasion. Hence, the very attribute that increases receiver receptivity works against the speaker in the end. Conversely, a less intelligent audience might understand with difficulty but will yield to persuasion more readily since they lack the ability to counterargue.

Self-esteem operates in the same manner as intelligence. An audience with high self-esteem will have confidence in its ability to understand the information. However, the self-confident audience will consider its beliefs as central to its character and will not yield to changes without much consideration. Audiences with low self-esteem will have trouble receiving the information, perhaps due to a lack of confidence in its ability to understand a given argument. At the same time, however, once the information is processed it yields to the argument easily in response to its own insecurity.

The involvement of the audience works in the same manner as intelligence and self-esteem. A highly involved audience, one which has a personal interest or investment in the subject, will readily receive the information because it feels "a need to know." Yet, because it has a vested interest in the subject, it will already have well-thought-out beliefs. Thus, changing these beliefs is a difficult task. An audience of low involvement will exhibit the opposite reactions. Low involvement can be translated into "not interested," which means that the audience will be paying attention to the information half-heartedly. Once the speaker can get the audience's attention long enough for the arguments to be received, the low involvement audience will easily yield because of its lack of emotional investment.

As opposed to high intelligence, self-esteem, and involvement, high anxiety makes an audience less likely to receive and understand information and more likely to yield to the information once it's understood. This phenomenon occurs due to the activity taking place in the minds of the audience. An audience that has high anxiety will be processing information (probably several pieces of information) at twice the speed of an audience with normal levels of anxiety. Thus, its ability to concentrate on a single persuasive argument will be greatly reduced. As a result of this mental state, an audience with high anxiety will easily agree to the argument (once it is received) because it will not take the time to question the information. An audience that has a low anxiety level will have the opposite response. Because its mind is in a relaxed state it will easily receive and understand the information. Unfortunately, this mental relaxation means the argument which was intended to be consciously bantered around received little, if any, mental attention. The end result is the reception of a lot of information but no effort to yield to it.

Yale Theory Application

Applying the Yale model, the Chief recognized his audience to be of high intelligence, high self-esteem, low involvement, and moderate anxiety. These characteristics dictate that the Chief will have to combat low reception due to the audience's low involvement and low yielding because of its high intelligence. And, therefore, he drew them emotionally into the subject by indicating their responsibility for the lives of the public and the police officers. Suddenly the lack of protective vests is not just a matter of concern for the police but the city council as well. After increasing its involvement, the Chief needed to increase the potential for yielding. An audience with high self-esteem will be more likely to yield to information if its self-perception is attacked. The Chief did this in his closing statement by implying that an intelligent audience would see the logic of the arguments and approve the proposal. In order to verify their intelligence and therefore protect their self-esteem, the council members should have felt compelled to yield. The only way to increase the yielding of a highly intelligent audience is to argue effectively, to use strong evidence, and to anticipate its counter-arguments. The Chief argued from ethos, logos, and pathos as demonstrated previously. He utilized powerful statistics from reputable sources. Likewise, he anticipated the counterarguments and addressed them by outlining the successful raffle held by another department. By the end of his speech, the council should have been highly receptive and yielding to the proposal in spite of the audience's original characteristics.

Conclusion

Theories of persuasion are often merely fancy titles used to describe what you and I do naturally everyday. The five theories discussed in this article are no different. Now that you have become familiarized with them, harness their power of persuasion and use it to your own advantage.

References

1. Douglas Ehninger, Bruce E. Gronbeck, and Alan H. Monroe, *Principles of Speech Communication,* 8th ed. (Glenview, Il.: Scott, Foresman and Company, 1980), pp. 245–255.
2. Abraham H. Maslow maintained that human beings are motivated to think, act, and respond as they do based upon different needs and wants. He categorized these needs and wants into a hierarchy: (1) Physiological, (2) Safety, (3) Belongingness and Love, (4) Esteem, and, (5) Self-actualization. According to Maslow, humans are unconsciously driven to satisfy these needs throughout their lives.
3. Ehninger, et al., pp. 245–246.
4. Ehninger, et al., p. 247.

5. Aristotle, *Rhetoric,* translated by Lane Cooper (New York: Appleton-Century, 1932).
6. Leon Festinger, *A Theory of Cognitive Dissonance* (Stanford, Ca.: Stanford University Press, 1957).
7. Musafer Sherif and Carl I. Hovland, *Social Judgment* (New Haven, Conn.: Yale University Press, 1961).
8. Carl I. Hovland, Irving L. Janis, and Harold H. Kelley, *Communication and Persuasion* (New Haven, Conn.: Yale University Press, 1953).

Answering Questions

9

Picture this situation: You've just finished delivering a well constructed speech, the audience has responded favorably, and now it's time for the inevitable question-and-answer (Q-and-A) period. While often neglected by many speakers in their preparation, this period should be one of the major concerns to all speakers. Why?

One of the laws of learning is the Law of Recency—people remember what was learned last: most recently. Since questions and answers normally come last, they're often best remembered, and the effects of a fine speech can be neutralized by poor performance during the Q-and-A period. Therefore, speakers should spend time preparing for questions as well as for the speech itself.

Here are some suggestions to help you handle those questions well:

Analyze the Audience

Surely, before you speak to any audience, you need to find out in detail just who they are. On an individual basis, that's impossible, but in the aggregate the job is much easier. Audiences are normally composed of people with a common background, usually focused on a particular issue. Some common thread runs through the audience—a cause or trait which has drawn them together, bonded them as a group, and brought them to listen to you. Experienced speakers identify that common thread and draw a profile of the audience's overall personality.

To help you profile any audience, here is just a sampling of questions to ask of the group's representative several weeks before you deliver your speech:

- How old are they?
- What's the gender mix: males to females?
- What is their socio-economic status?
- What is their educational level?
- Has anyone from a similar department ever spoken to them before?
- What topics seem to go over well with the group?

- What attitudes about you, your department, and the topic do they hold?
- What values or beliefs are important to them?
- What is the audience's cultural and ethnic background?
- Why are they meeting?
- What are the group/organization's stated goals and principles?
- Where will the speech be delivered?
- Who else may be speaking?
- What time of day will you be speaking?

Brainstorm Possible Questions

Few people are clairvoyant, but you'll be surprised how well you can anticipate questions if you've analyzed the audience and are willing to brainstorm possible questions. To brainstorm, simply focus on the topic and allow ideas about it to surface freely and uncensored. Forget how wild or bizarre the ideas may seem—get them out first. You can always cut back later. To enhance your ideas, ask a few of your staff or colleagues to join you for a brainstorming session. Give them the speech topic and the audience's background and then let them go to work. Designate a recorder to list the ideas on a chalkboard or piece of paper. Don't ridicule any ideas—just let them come as quickly as the recorder can write them down. Review the list, rephrase the ideas as questions, and place the questions in priority order. The result: A list which will serve as a starting point.

Next, answer the questions. Some speakers list a few key words; others write out the entire answer to better evaluate its quality and completeness. Obviously, you would never read the answer to an audience; however, writing out the answer beforehand allows you to take stock before, not after the speech. This technique often will cover most of the questions you'll be asked. Thus, you'll be as prepared for the questions as you are for the speech itself.

Listen Actively to Questions

When someone from the audience asks a question, pretend you're a reporter under a deadline, and you'll be able to comprehend questions more accurately and quickly. Reporters listen intently because they have to accurately report the facts which they are given only one brief chance to absorb. So, mentally assume you're only going to get that single chance at the question.

Once asked, quickly repeat the question in your mind. This repetition will just take a microsecond but will increase comprehension measurably. Next, repeat the question out loud to the questioner. Why? For the following reasons:

- First, to make sure you understand the question correctly. A simple nod or affirming look from the questioner will help you assess your comprehension.
- Second, to allow the rest of the audience to hear the question. Few things frustrate audiences more than hearing an answer without knowing the question.
- Third, to give you more time to think about your answer. Buying even a few seconds, especially for critical questions, will prove invaluable.

Talk to the Entire Audience

After you've repeated the question directly to the questioner, address your answer to the entire audience, not just to the questioner. This accomplishes two important things. First, involving the entire audience by maintaining eye contact with them helps you keep them all interested and alert. Second, you'll avoid being monopolized by follow-up questions from the same person, thus preventing the rest of the audience from feeling neglected.

Define Terms Up Front

When you're asked a question which contains words or terms you're unfamiliar with, be sure to ask the questioner for definitions before launching into your answer. Chances are better than even that others in the audience have the same difficulty with the question and will mentally thank you for clarifying it. Definitions also force the questioner to be specific which prevents vague questions and even vaguer answers.

Be cautious in defining values as well as words. If someone asks whether a particular thing is good or bad, you'll have to clarify that person's standards or values. For example, rain might be considered a godsend to those experiencing a drought, but a curse to those in the midst of a flood. Get definitions and values clarified to accurately answer questions.

Divide Multiple Questions

Some people like to ask multiple questions threaded together into one confusing and awkward question. For example, "What is your position on widgits?; how did you come to invent your first widgit?; and why does your company continue to pollute the environment by making widgits?" To defend against these situations, divide and conquer. Answer the portion of the question you're most comfortable with first. Next, ask the questioner to repeat the rest of the question. Sometimes you'll find he or she can't remember the entire question. In any case, by breaking up the question into its component parts, you'll be able to focus on each part individually, thus avoiding the confusion inherent in such questions.

Be Brief and to the Point

Remember the audience has already sat through your speech and the clock is still ticking. When you answer questions, don't burden the audience with long monologues—give them precise responses to allow more people the opportunity to ask questions. Further, understand that the more you ramble, the further from the point you'll stray. And if you do so in critical speeches, you'll find yourself swimming into unfamiliar and dangerous waters. Remember, if you can't be good, be brief; and, if you can be good *and* brief, you'll be great!

Support Your Opinions with Evidence

An opinion with no evidence is merely an assertion, but one backed with evidence becomes a defendable argument. Credibility can only come when you offer solid evidence to back up your opinions or claims. If you claim widgets are the best on the market, you have to tell the audience why. For example, "My widgits are the best on the market because they last longer, are more efficient, and cost less than any comparable product." If you've accurately analyzed the audience and they hold these values, you've provided the kind of evidence which will support your claim.

Admit When You Don't Know

When you don't know an answer, admit it. Then follow right up with, "But if you'll give me your phone number later, I'll find out the answer and get back to you." People can accept that you don't know all the answers, but they will never accept a lack of candor.

Remember, if you tell someone you'll get back to them, do so promptly. If you don't, your reputation will suffer immensely. People keep track of public promises and the word will spread quickly if you don't keep yours.

Place Limits

When you're the speaker, you're in charge, and the audience has certain expectations. For example, if a person asks a question which turns into a monologue, the audience will nonverbally signal by shuffling feet, shifting positions or whispering to indicate their displeasure. You need to set some limits. To do so, you might say, "Excuse me, what exactly is your question?" Nail down the question. The audience will respect you for efficiency or condemn you for inaction.

You also need to limit the length of time you'll accept questions. When you sense the Q-and-A period has lasted long enough, have a predesignated signal for your host. Use an agreed upon head nod or subtle hand gesture to indicate your desire to end the questions. At that point, your host should announce that there will only be time for one more question. As an alternative, you can make that same announcement yourself. In either case you'll place a limit, and the audience will respect it, particularly if it's a reasonable one and if they've had sufficient time to ask probative questions about your topic.

Avoid Arguments

Avoid arguing with or embarrassing people in front of an audience or it will backfire on you. Every speaker has positional authority when in front of an audience—by tradition the speaker is in charge. When that positional authority is used to steamroller people in the audience, however, invariably the others will sympathize with them. When you disagree, be firm, but say it with a smile. For example: "I'm sorry, sir, that was not what I meant to say. Perhaps there's been a slight misunderstanding. I said. . . ."

Rephrase Certain Questions

Some people like to ask volatile questions, and such inflammatory questions are better left unrepeated or rephrased. For example, "Are your widgets still unsafe for children?" No answer to such a question would be prudent, and repeating it would only confirm the implication made by the questioner.

Merely rephrase such questions to your advantage: "The question deals with product safety, so let me tell you about all the controls we use to insure a durable and safe product which has earned us awards from consumer councils around the nation." In this example, you've taken the sting out of the question and answered it positively.

Answering questions from an audience can cap off a well-delivered speech or undermine it. Though often left to chance, questions are as inevitable and predictable as the speech itself. By employing these tips, you'll make answering questions a natural and interesting part of your speech—a part which will enhance the speech and the speaker.

III
COMMUNICATING IN SPECIAL SITUATIONS

Communicating in a Crisis

10

Introduction

Sometimes we have to communicate under stressful conditions. And none are more stressful than hostage cases, where communication is not just a matter of budgets or promotions, rather it involves the safety of human life. Further, in the midst of communicating with hostage takers, police agencies must simultaneously communicate with the ever-present news media, representing the people's right to know. How we communicate to the media in these situations can not only affect the safety of the hostages, but also our future image with the public we serve.

Being prepared for the media in such situations requires police departments to prethink strategies for handling such communication dilemmas. This article offers some practical solutions to these difficult, yet predictable situations.

The Problem—Communication Breakdown

The lone hostage taker sat with his eyes riveted to a television set which he had demanded during tedious negotiations with police and the FBI. He was ready to surrender when the sight of police snipers moving into defensive positions flashed across the screen. Now feeling threatened, he balked at his previous offer to surrender, and negotiations continued for another day.

The conduct of the news media at hostage scenes has become a major concern for law enforcement. This concern has been heightened by the recent upsurge in world-wide terrorism. While the United States has only experienced a few terrorist situations, numerous hostage-taking incidents have filled the headlines of American newspapers.

Since the terrorist often takes a hostage to negotiate his demands, the terms "terrorism" and "hostage taking" are often used interchangeably. However, thse terms are distinct, since many hostage sit-

Reprinted with Permission from the *FBI Law Enforcement Bulletin,* September, 1979, Title: "The Hostage/Terrorist Situation and the Media."

uations are the result of a criminal caught in the act rather than a premeditated plan, and many terrorist activities do not involve hostages. The term "hostage/terrorist situation" can be used to describe hostage taking by terrorists and nonpolitical criminals.

The hostage taker, whether political or not, creates a dramatic forum for his demands: Life and death are in the balance; the outcome is suspenseful; there are victims, weapons, and emotions; and in many cases, there is a message for the world. All the elements are present for a lead story. Says one reporter about a hostage taker in Cleveland, "They paid attention to him because of his terrorism."[1] Dr. George Gebner, Dean of the Annenberg School of Communications, describes these acts as media events without which terrorists couldn't exist. He questions to what extent media wants to cooperate with terror.[2] Halina Czerniejewski wrote in *The Quill*, "The act of covering a news event changes the character of the event. . . . This leaves news media in a curious and uncomfortable position—that of wanting to be observers, but inadvertently or advertently becoming participants—as victims or vehicles."[3]

Fierce competition for the story tends to draw more media personnel and intensifies the coverage which results. "It's often the local news competition that compels journalists, maneuvering for each minute-to-minute scoop, to get in the way of police," reports Robert Merey of the *National Observer*.[4] In the scramble for news and the competition for scoops, the broadcast media can make mistakes.[5] This competition creates problems for law enforcement personnel at the scene. Such was the situation with one case in Cleveland, Ohio. A reporter for a local television station called the news producer and told him that the situation appeared to be ending. The producer, wanting to be the first with the story, went live via "mini-cam" with pictures of police snipers readying their defensive positions on the surrounding rooftops. The hostage taker, who had access to a television, saw the positioning of snipers and balked. He shouted, "Everything is off, right now." In fact, negotiations went on for at least another day. The chief of police later said that the drama would have ended a day earlier had that mini-cam incident not occurred.[6]

Advancements in technology, like the mini-cam, have posed problems for law enforcement and media alike. Truly an electronic marvel, the mini-cam or portable camera allows live broadcasts from almost anywhere; hence, it gets the story as it happens. Unfortunately, this can be dangerous in a hostage/terrorist situation. Virgil Dominic, news director of a Cleveland television station, stated, "The portable camera is a wonderful tool. But we are just learning how to use it."[7] The incident described above prompted this news director to reconsider his station's coverage of such events. Dominic said it was his feeling that the competitiveness of attracting a larger audience caused the error in judgment of showing the snipers prematurely. The ultimate decision of that station was to not cover such events live in the future. Dominic entreated other local television news directors to follow suit and where lives are at stake, to defuse the competitive nature of these incidents.

Similar situations have generated much discussion between media and police. A recent study conducted by Dr. Michael Sommer at California State University at Northridge entitled, "Project on Media Coverage of Terrorism," surveyed police chiefs and media representatives from the 30 largest cities in the United States. The report contains some divergent opinions on the role of the media in hostage/terrorist situations, and though some of the responses are predictable, others are surprising. Television directors agreed that live coverage is not a good idea, although they still hold that the decision should be based on the individual case. Concerning journalists' conversations with terrorists, a plurality of radio, television, and print media agreed that prior police consent was the way to proceed.[8]

Some of the more sober comments have come from the media itself. Tom Becherer of Detroit's WWJ-TV stated, "There is a difference, I think, between the public's right to know and the public's right to know everything."[9] Says Wayne Vriesman of WGN-TV, Chicago, "I will never black out a story. That would lead the public to think we will black out other stories. I would draw the line, though, on passing on police plans to a terrorist. . . ."[10] This discussion within the media has caused it to take a closer look at itself and its actions during these events. As a result, network guidelines have been promulgated.

CBS was the first network to draw up guidelines for its news staffs regarding hostage/terrorist situations. The guidelines, though they leave certain questions unanswered, do show a sensitivity for not only the hostage but also law enforcement. NBC likewise has written guidelines, as has the United Press International whose guidelines put particular emphasis on establishing procedures at each local station for the coverage of such events. This raises the often-echoed complaint that network and headquarters-type edicts don't hold much water in the individual area stations. Local stations do not want to be locked into a formal set of rules established by network executives which may not allow any flexibility in individual cases.

Guidelines do have some drawbacks. An author for *The Quill* comments,

> The problem will be to come up with guidelines which will be flexible enough so as not to encroach on news judgment, thoughtful enough to deal with the complexities of the situation and clear enough to help newspeople deal reasonably with fast breaking, tense life-and-death situations.[11]

Jim Warren, a reporter for KPHO-TV, Phoenix, believes one basic guideline is that the media work closely with the authorities.[12] Norman S. Hartman, news director of KOVR, Sacramento, says that guidelines "can serve a useful purpose to get newspeople thinking and talking about news coverage during such incidents."[13]

Ron Tindiglia of ABC News, New York, sees media's role, that of a disseminator of news, as a vital one demanding great responsibilities to reduce vulnerability against manipulations.[14] Dan Rather of CBS News says in support, "When violent people are playing to the camera, there's no question that the medium itself can become a kind of hostage, and the reporter has to dodge and struggle to keep from being captured and used."[15]

The police and media in such hostage/terrorist situations need not be antagonists. In fact, the news media at different times has helped resolve the hostage taker's demands. Such was the case in Cleveland when a police captain and a 17-year-old female employee of the police department were taken hostage in 1977. The hostage taker refused to talk to police negotiators and would only discuss his situation with a local black television reporter. Under the guidance of police, the reporter talked the hostage taker out of the situation, and no one was injured.

A danger arises, however, when media personnel decide to become "freelance" negotiators with the perpetrators, as in the Hanafi Muslim's hostage taking in Washington, D.C. Hamaas Khaalis, leader of the sect, was interviewed on the air concerning the question of whether or not he could trust the police.[16] This question obviously makes the job of negotiation—which is based on trust—a much more difficult one. In another interview, Khaalis was asked whether he had set any deadlines yet. The last thing a negotiator ever wants is a deadline.[17]

Law enforcement has had its problems adapting to the hostage/terrorist situation and its relationship to the press. The initial reaction to a hostage/terrorist crisis is to direct all manpower to the tactical and negotiating efforts to free hostages safely, to the exclusion of all else, even the media. The neglect of the media by law enforcement in its all-out efforts to save lives often creates additional problems. The New York City Police Department (NYPD) discovered this phenomenon in its first hostage negotiation case at a sporting goods store in Brooklyn. After the Munich Olympics, the NYPD formed a hostage negotiations team in 1972 under the direction of Dr. Harvey Schlossberg and Capt. Frank Bolz. When the Brooklyn incident broke, the police wanted a news blackout and went so far as to shut off the electric power to the entire area. The media countered by setting up portable generators and floodlights, which inadvertently served to silhouette the police and leave the perpetrators in the shadows. Having learned a lesson from this experience, the NYPD now spends time with the media, to the point of including them in its hostage training sessions.[18]

The Solution—The Public Information Officer

Communication between media and law enforcement tends to strengthen the trust between the two. As one police chief stated in a nationwide survey, "On-scene liaison between police and media and a policy of department-wide openness promote a climate of mutual trust and understanding wherein the police and the media can fulfill their respective obligations to the public."[19] The time for communication with the media, however, comes long before the crisis occurs. The chief of police in Warrensville Heights, Ohio, who was involved in a hostage/terrorist situation, says that until that crisis he had never really spent a whole lot of time with members of the media. Now he believes in establishing an ongoing relationship with them. "The key is common sense and cooperation between media and law enforcement," said the FBI Special Agent in Charge during the Warrensville Heights Case.[20] Building a good rapport with the media—one based on forthrightness, openness, and trust—long before the hostage taker ever strikes is a necessity.

Essential to this trust relationship is a public information officer (PIO). Each police department should have some individual assigned the duty of liaison with the press, and that person should be someone other than the chief. The PIO gives the chief the latitude he needs to run the department and still be available for press conferences and media appearances, while the PIO has daily contact with the press to handle the usual inquiries common to most police departments. The PIO should disseminate public information to the media and remain sensitive to the needs of the press in day-to-day operations and especially during a crisis situation.

In the FBI, Special Agents have been appointed as media representatives in each of the FBI's 59 field offices. All the media representatives are trained in press relations at in-service training sessions held at the FBI Academy. Media representatives have served the FBI, the press, and the American public well, and they become particularly important during a hostage/terrorist situation.

Before a hostage/terrorist situation occurs, the PIO and the chief should take the initiative to meet with the video, radio, and print media, including the wire services. These meetings should involve a discussion with the news director, city editors, and supervisors of reporters concerning the nature of hostage negotiations and the problems associated with them. Several departments, notably the NYPD, have been very successful with this technique. As Captain Bolz put it, "We try to take away the mystique."[21] The press must see that law enforcement is sincere in attempting to balance the people's right to know with the protection of lives. Often, a general presentation to the media by the department's hostage negotiator and the PIO helps to create an awareness and sensitivity to law enforcement's problems.

When the crisis situation comes, the PIO should be one of the first on the scene. His job at the scene is to ascertain immediately the facts and report to the media the who, what, when, where, why, and how of the situation in a general briefing. In this way the entire press corps can get the truth from a reliable police official, hopefully eliminating the need for freelancing by the media.

After the initial press briefing, the PIO should establish a media command post. This post should serve as a centralized area from which press statements can be made, information released, and questions answered. The location depends on each situation. It may be 50 feet or 5,000 feet away from the incident; it may be outdoors or on another floor in the same building where the hostages are being held. Location of the media command post should be accessible, while not intruding or interfering with tactical police or negotiators. However, it should not be at such an unreasonable distance away from the scene so as to invite freelancing. The ideal media command post should have outside telephone lines for the press to call in their stories, toilet facilities, and if possible, a place to sit down or even lie down, as some cases go on for days.

During the hostage/terrorist situation, the PIO serves as a direct link between law enforcement and the media. His or her job is not only to keep the press informed, but also to buffer the command post from the pressures of the media, so that the chief or commanding officer can concentrate on the job at hand and not be tied up with external interruptions. Finally, the PIO should remain with the media at all times. Since many situations take days to resolve, consideration should be given to having an alternate PIO.

Proper handling of news media at a hostage/terrorist situation not only requires scheduling and coordination, but also a delicate balance between the duty of the press to inform and of law enforcement to protect. This is not an easy task; however, the problems can be worked out with mutual effort on the part of both law enforcement and the media.

References

1. David Abbott and Sergio Lalli, "The Media Captured Along with the Hostages," *Sunday Plain Dealer Magazine,* May 8, 1977, p. 34.
2. Carey Winfrey, "Hanafi Seizure Fans New Debate on Press Coverage of Terrorists," *The New York Times,* March 19, 1977, p. 33.
3. Halina J. Czerniejewski, "Guidelines for the Coverage of Terrorism," *The Quill,* July–August 1977, p. 21.
4. Robert W. Merry, "On-the-Air Hindrance? Broadcasters Search Souls Over Coverage," *The National Observer,* April 22, 1977.
5. John Weisman, "When Hostages' Lives are at Stake . . . Should a T.V. Reporter Push On or Pull Back?" *TV Guide Magazine,* August 26, 1978, p. 5.
6. Abbott and Lalli, p. 32.
7. Abbott and Lalli, p. 33.
8. "Study Concludes There's Not Much Agreement Between Police and the Media Officials," *Variety,* (Hollywood, California) August 17, 1978, p. 1.
9. "T.V. Newsmen Split on Air Time for Terrorists," *More,* June 1977, p. 20.
10. Ibid.
11. Ernie Schultz, "Censorship Is No Solution to Coverage of Terrorist-Hostage Situation," *RTNDX Communicator,* July 1977, p. 7.
12. *More,* p. 20.
13. "Many Stations Enact Guidelines on Involvement with Terrorists," *Television/Radio Age,* October 21, 1977, p. 26.
14. Ibid, p. 74.
15. Ibid.
16. Weisman, p. 5.
17. Ibid.
18. Ibid, p. 6.
19. "Police Chiefs Blame TV for Acts of Terrorism," *Editor and Publisher,* August 27, 1977, p. 12.
20. Abbott and Lalli, p. 33.
21. Weisman, p. 6.

Notes

Notes

Notes